Shades of Light:

A Triumph of City

by

M. A. Coghill

Published by
City of Poetry Ltd

Published in The United Kingdom in 2012 by
www.cityofpoetry.co.uk

Printed in Great Britain by Shortrunpress Ltd

A CIP catalogue record for this book is available from the British Library
ISBN: 978-0-9573510-0-4
Cover Design: © M. A. Coghill

Contents

LOVE

Seriatim

Dead wood word unread or line for
this spine responds for the first time
thoughts rise seep along a smooth stem
the soft calyx opens backwards

first showing lacking full colour
soft exploration picking out
first rasp of a finger on leaves
examine the contents growing

quiet breathing suspense intense
successive or there will maybe
possibilities open out
suffusion in thoughts and perhaps

chances petals unfold plot lines
genus bright then sere leaves blowing
press in code to soft snap closure
good ah seriatim more and

OPOS AFFAIR

(I do not wait long) for the call[1]
running down towards the bridge
to meet you as arranged

springing forward on a spike of static
the rules are in place
shock shock under the roar of traffic

mouthing words between rushing
speeding towards the tube racketing
beguiling new reality beckoning

but carved from the same old icons
takatakatakatakataka
'follow the woman you meet at the
entrance'

it's with all-round element of trust
I think here tish whish tishha whish
the next move as - follow instructions

and when you ring in
'please enter your security code'
reality adrenalin up against

being asked to do the impossible
in public 'pick up your message'
'we have GPS on you out in the open'

I'm in the virtual shadow now
exploit the hiding places
nothing but the real laden breathing

real panic - forgetting life's a game
do not cross here if you want real -
opos-ed GPS my best friend now

tic toc tica toc tica tica
ground floor mind the doors
press one for.....two for....

all done by command or evasion of orders
opos awol
ramp up to 119 beats per minute

there is real blood on the floor
by the door panting please help me
the phone like a leach in the hand

I take *opos* advantage of the shadow
the endgame tube station entrance
escalator swish *opos* descending

the clock starts ticking its duration
of suspense all over again
'your GPS is out there and lonely'

'it's the imperfections that are interesting'
these lcds are mine
isotropic elongated nema[2]

Anomie vs Logic Gates[3]

when I look at the next moment
I am somewhere else
measuring the rhythm of dislocation
contiguity replaces effort at
narrative is of
environmental interest testing
the copper connections of
this building imprints heat
grey windows gleam grey static
padded footsteps
in the communal corridor
an adjusted fire door thuds to
'vortex central!'
some abstract connection in
city smells of white noise
this man walks stares straight ahead
breath, tube, sulphur, CO_2
"Anomie!"
why I can still breathe!
in the maelstrom of movement
the door opens and bang he falls crashing to
the platform head first
from the London bound train
there by 3 gone by 4 out by 5
generic life = specific place +anomie
and the derived total
is one or nought and not or
this is a delightful reduction of purpose

IO

pushes past combinations of time
gloss past the winter's afternoon
nothing is yawning
I should have taken the children out
watching them squabble over a game
aiaiai how the clock ticks
voices rise/fall rain beats/patters
tea toast/biscuits mmm/oioi
cobwebs across the eyes of maenads
leaving Pound's exquisite beauty
whilst we humdrum flesh out ioioio
until the hourglass turns aiai
stirs the air with purpose
the light is going the room needs heat
turn on the light/fire off on and/or
what digits measure the contentment
rewards and deprivations
the frenzy of the past week and
putting the kettle on/units tumble
combinations and random clusters
eureka shouted within earshot
'put that down!' (and/or)(and/not)
the positive charge is not considered
twist decode elongate correlate
sub-divide again (and/not)(not/yet)
handle all microns with exquisite care
'I have walked down streets that echo
the same footsteps time after time'
gates do not open in *this* way

Top Rhemes and Pavement Themes

assumptions quickly
voices drowned by the bus reversing
the anxiety that this person is violent
'Get to Holborn'
that way go that way
the door red lights the hoodie quickly
takes
the baked beans
does not pay
imperceptible movement of air
(I see them sitting)
(Where the sign says)
Coffee
(I see their mouths move)
talking unheard through traffic
(I see one) take
new cheap trainers from his jacket
(I see them) thrown
(He mouths) ok here you are
'I got them for you'
(I understand)
[they're ok then]
the next day I walk past as the bus pulls away
this time a packet of sandwiches falls
free real stolen - a three rheme sandwich

The Poet Listens in on the Eidometropolis[4]

this friend not used to the city
asking me to do the unacceptable
drive into and out of the city centre
twice in one day taking instructions:
you will not do the same thing twice
not notice your immediate
surroundings -
eidoindividual
who is female born here by chance
don't visit galleries
don't travel on the tube for years
shut down the options
become home based it's safer
except neighbours turned out to be -
eidosequence
I arrange to meet you at the V&A
'I've got your birthday present'
and later you said
'what a lovely present'
I remembered the seat
the sunlight through glass
I didn't see you again -
eidoevent
stop dead by the petrol station
under the plane tree I am sure
I hear the most beautiful recording ever
a bird sings falling like honey on soul
forgetting my errand
gradually the late summer evening
city night air eidodawns
this is the nightingale
high up in the street lining plane tree

undertowed by cars
sound falling through dust
Keats would have died for this
the eidoquality sound
madness inappropriately
no-one stopping looking up
I was stared at
so the meaning changes
slight invasion in what garden
eidocreak crack one word of warning
a blackbird cries
break break break
one step further and
the silence breaks
creak crack creak
interface between speakers
password: ay2zed
speak speak speak
break break break

Love You to Pieces

long legs in ads
reality body image pixelated
avenues of thought
shards of netting
snagging on wind and broken glass
specifically with gender analysis seen
in the window of the empty house
we are building blocks
for everyone to make money
but our lives are fragmented
we are disassembled bricks
cracked lumps of cement

we are the undeveloped
parts plus parts of city estates
forgotten families on the top floors
disembodied facial expressions
breeze blocks render glass tiles
uneven pavements
litter on the stairs
we are demands that are not met
push prams in awkward places
sullen expressions
smiles in odd moments
silences at inappropriate times
incomplete panoramas
the sound of combinations of voices
taking apart the pieces attempting
to balance the parts overbearing

Declamatory Mrs Gilpin[5]

Politician: firstly let us address the issues of gender and city, poverty and wealth, whether there is poetry of universal appeal, a poetry of self and identity, a poetry that addresses the issues of safety and danger, how this is going to be read in the venue that has been booked?
Administrators raggedly shuffle papers.
Poet: no one is talking about being paid. Who will pay for it?
Philosopher: the politician - that's a joke
Poet: if the strings are tied I can't perform I can't write.
Politician: we have set up an independent organisation that vets everyone to the point of exclusion before we pay them a very little just to egg them on but everyone here will speak for nothing.
Adminstrators smile happily
Philosopher looks grim
Poet: words or grim is that all you can do? Here I am working my guts out coming up with new forms and patterns and you are not engaging.
Semiotician: I maintain that wherever you go I can follow.
In breezes the critic who is warmly welcomed by the publisher and by the poet who is a sycophant at heart
Critic: have you room for me?
Poet: the semiotician keeps driving a wedge between me and all my parts.

I write and formulate and rewrite and reformulate, there is barely more than the pleasure of it - do you feel my need? (thinking of emotions and garrets)
Politician: you, the poet, have skills at your fingertips and you need educational opportunities for this
Administrators make notes
Poet: and emotions high emotions
Philosopher: what is the purpose of poetry?
Publisher (sarcastic): why you make money out of it (as he takes a call from his printer – who is refusing to print the text until paid).
The semiotician is filling in a chart
Poet: are these signs metaphors?
The philosopher looks disapproving
Administrators frown.
Mrs Gilpin (in tears): emotions are the vessels of inspiration
Philosopher: inspiration has its place but you need to control your words
Mrs Gilpin: no no it's the space
Philosopher: not a single bit of it has defined parameters
Politican shrugs.
Critic: dramatisation of information encourages debate
Philosopher: a foundation stone for inspiration is formed by as yet unrecognised signs funnelling their way to the surface of the mind as words.
Semiotician: I couldn't agree more – if only I could label more of them and faster as you speak
Poet: I do not understand myself -

form is required and the purpose is to glorify;
is to record; is to explore the self (dead end?);
is to give pleasure (and more or less).
Critic: you deliberately set out to
overdetermine confuse
Poet: no! no!
Critic: and it's just that there are members of
the public who like poems as crosswords
Poet: oh! oh!
Critic: high emotion state occasion
promulgation of morality - temperance, virtue?
Poet: well at the very least I like to push
outwards the limits of meaning in words and
their combinations
Semiotician: this is fascinating.
Politician: but who benefits? We cannot
condescend.
Semiotician (looks up from searching the
programme): there is no logic
Administrators get out highlighters.
Poet: torque it's all torque the topic is tropes I
have to learn the tropes tra la disintegration of
thought is never far away we need more to go
on
Philosopher: mimesis and diegesis, remember
the words mean something
Critic files fingernails. Poet files words
Politician: we really want to nail this one
Semiotician: the parings are somethings
Critic: it seems to me that poets are unable to
state their position clearly
Philosopher: terms need to be more black and
white, it's the control

Poet: oh you mean performance, patterns, the silences, synapses ending in shouting and analepses with the times
Philosopher: we have started with assumptions
Poet: we have suggested turns of phrase
rhymes and figures of speech -
you have discarded so much
Semiotician (rapidly typing out labels): this is even more fascinating
Critic (edgy): how? why?
Publisher: I certainly can't sell *that* to a new market
Poet: you mean the editor? professor of poetry?
Politician: what you are proposing is elitist. Well if you want funding you can't go back to the classics.
Coffee time as the room clears to a backdrop of scraping chairs. The Administrators rush and take all the coffee and tea provided.
Mrs Gilpin (longingly): this is flying past me again and again - mimesis comes naturally to me but you prefer to record, recall, evoke through naturalism and identification with subject. In this guise is poetry fiction? Is the target less dramatic when diegetic? Is drama regarded as traffic between stage and auditorium (not audience?), and the spectator understands words from the poet's mouth; empathy from declamation, suspension of disbelief. Are we to imagine a world as real but always there between empathy and the poet?
Critic (interrupts): 'criticism is stimulated with reference to the way empathy is generated, not

with reference to the incidents the spectator
sees reproduced on the stage'[6] (by the poet).
Mrs Gilpin: erect scaffolding -
Politician: Oh hustings! Oh hustings!
Mrs Gilpin: articulate empathy,
put in some lyrics, tropes, techniques,
naturalistic events. We understand the poet to
be witness? The words are more important
than the poet even though the poet wrote them.
The meaning may well rush past us both on the
outward and return journey.
Semiotician: so we are talking about a double
layering, words and meaning, story,
significance, signs!
Mrs Gilpin: yes and up and down the lines back
and forth across the patterns in and out of
levels of reference!
The Administrators leave empty cups.
The Semiotician accepts a lucrative contract
from advertising.
The Poet lays all bare to the empty hall.

The Poet Performs: Love is a "fat gold watch"[7]

and there is no room for viewpoints
gravity pulls everything together
or force of air expands to fit
lost in a flashback tied to this routine
the day drip feeds unrelated place
and predominant time causes lesions
space comes from hope I was born
here
access denied
for allowing a life of mindless irony
or the endless performance vantage
is merely the darkness the fourth wall
cheeks kissed hand presses shoulder
come and meet us all
the belonging moment
I can hardly remember my cues
alas! alas! amock! amock! *access denied*
set up a stage re-set the perspective
passions rise against the rushing tide
hot tunnel air pushes homeward
trying to extract essential control
I have learnt my lines interpreted
emotions with the opening scene
where the young woman is accosted
by addicts in the park assailed
by normal exigencies taken
swerving action and in the last scenes
taking the opportunity of my last lines to
demonstrate that dramatic justice is finely
balanced and gives satisfaction to your vantage
point corruption…
access denied

the rest of the cast break into song:
John Gilpin was a trading man
who raced by fast - off course
we ought to wait for his return
but his code and timing's false
I feel lost in the city today
determination as primeval force
pitting itself against timetables
phone calls booking forms diaries
the explorer leaves lists of provisions
a diary of preparation for each day
going on an expedition
access denied
what is this voice which calls from a
blanket of silence
like the trails of traffic seen from the
hill in the park
glinting in a setting sun on the north
bound motorway
and the approaching headlights like
stars spinning
molecular chains gleaming with
promise of revelation -
'I know….how love cries and calls
and will not be shut out with doors
nor walls'[8]
night hours spent awake in bed
nursing words breast fed
'Gall tempered with honey, this is the
lover's song'[9]
speaking to me in the dark marches
of the night
turning on the light commanding
'write!'

how simple when there is the real
baby to feed
the readers cry 'we own the text'
but the real text is a crowded poet's
hypotext
and she, in the audience cried out
something in the poem about a
mother's death
that hit her solar plexus hard
poems receive rapturous applause
adjust to the different light
the gendering is complete
the false premise is
access denied
voices of maenads readers anyone
the sacrifice comes back to me
with such force I cannot but weep
(hypoweep you understand)
whilst half asleep
'I know how Love can roar throughout the
mind'[10]

Passion in the Perishadow

at work in a room that faces due south
and the windows onto the main road
shut to keep out the noise and air echoed by the
air conditioning grinding limping its way
through a tired afternoon desperate
we open the office door pin back
the fierce fire hinge with a chair
sit very still to avoid an all over sweat
real time hovers with the strip lighting
breaks out of the shadows

walking home through the swish of tyres
wet tarmac and pulses of light
punching holes in sodium glow
rain throwing spattered lights splitting
half reflections gritty puddles
whichever way the light fixes scoops
intersecting circles in deepening
shadow
touched by an embrace of occlusion
wet feet wet hands fumbling for keys
swallowed by lesser noise
now the front door is shut
but this one returns
impassioned desperate shrieks
haunt impale the air
'Oh God, Oh God, Oh God no, NO'
the woman driving away from the
courts
with the car windows wound down gasping
fighting to breathe -
We are a circle of turning witness

trauma whipping past in rhetoric
shortness of breath punched from the
mind

now standing facing north east
the brief sun on a winter's morning
frost over the station roof gleams
tall buildings cast long shadows hint
slight warmth just before catching
the corner wind, cutting, chastening
in alleyways and rat-runs, pushes
us twisters from hot air vents
elegant clear sky light hovers
the stalest cooking fat in the world
(also burnt) recycling hot moist
foetid in our hair teased
strange microbes with sensual strobes
compelling passion
floreating through blood skin
nerve endings breathing touch me
be touched wanting to know more
and tomorrow between midnight
and midnight lovers do not
track time watch only the infinite
movements of their beloved
caressed by a thousand breaths
scintillated by a thousand sights
the intimacy is extreme –
eternity to just now

Memo: Take this letter to Mr Eliot –

DISCIPLINE

please take care please hold the handrail
while travelling Caution moving conveyer
Measure the movement of a body

Boolean Term

The lighting can be manually adjusted
and the thermostat gives us perfect
conditions.
Tap, tap. Do not switch on when
empty then open
a window on a world in brown and
black and white:
this money has changed colour; an aid
when red.
We volunteered to this rising, now dig
out
the apple tree and survive one orange
sunset
gem, hanging in the balance - may give
a tableau
of grief somewhere, not mine. No
pasaran! Tuesday
pulls out a war of attrition. On paper it
looks as if an interview isn't to this
end.
Travelling by guillotine to a silent open
unaccompanied by hell holes fast
forwarded:
this is clear control of a kind, the remit
cedes.
You are entering a red zone: the

Caution moving conveyer please take care
please hold the handrail while travelling
she has fallen her shopping awry

Memo: His sibyl supported by caryatids:

billboards are
available with red foods for your
protection.
Investments can go down as well as up
- oh! This
garden was venerated for centuries
and the
aroma is very distinctive. With
cutbacks,
innovation sports in lane two but you
can't
see over the bridge: let this anger bring
you much
closer to me in time capsules with cod
liver
fortunate oil - cross my palm and let
there be change
all day breakfast eaten here due to
vandalism
on the tracks. This is a cowardly act, I
say
to you: sign appeal for witnesses, last
Sunday,
deconstruct the angle: if you can read
this you're
too close and sound your horn. Cough
without drowsiness.
Private. Remote control doors open

moving conveyer please take care please hold the handrail while travelling Caution
Caution moving in time in relation to herself

Memo: 'Our duties may be monotonous, but they cannot properly be described as mechanical'

heart in ice;
disadvantageously we replay coercions
of intimate moments fading into light-
time:
record for training purposes. Memo:
Warning!
Personal; but crack this dress code.
Date force sell out:
one careful employer takes out all fine
line breaks.
Read nervously and smile please,
every picture
reshuffles the trial posture in a sitting.
The ambiance; second fold, believe this
and you'll -
try again later; take two, look down,
redefine
leaving guarantees we cannot dredge
out before
Go: wait while lift to fifth floor power to the
'Ha!'

conveyer please take care please hold the handrail while travelling Caution moving
her purse agape oranges roll steadily down

Dure

transition patterns differences
response *this same* person *that* shop -
by tube or pedestrians dogs barking -
in the lobby – where is the hearing?
the security arch bleeps I wait
I know that the process of city
is the eradication of waiting
which is only for lower forms of life
transition that takes us to troglodyte
the chairs cause natural slouching
grit against slump
the chairman is over polite and is
nervous when physically approached
moving through impact process denial
deriving ergonomic measure life
brutalised from the first for many years
a brute a tupt[12] a dure or just a blow
suffered 3 blows today 10 score tupt
going to appeal a 20 dure score
after 20 years in the city score
may well be 20,000 we need to
concertina up devalue the noughts
20k dures debased to 200
a nightdure a daydure a dureffect
my cold catches up with me
I cough through highways usage

please take care please hold the handrail
while travelling Caution moving conveyer
not by the number of times willing

desperately sip water suck pastilles
the woman with the greasy complexion
and bright red lipstick entirely controls
responses legally imitative
she walks through detractions implies
she might have to ask for costs a wave
of anxiety in the pen-pusher ranks
the chair's loose suit rustles over his shanks
she drives her point with adroit shuffling
I think I would willingly have a stand up
slanging match with Miss Grease Face
and her client
with the big red face red handkerchief
his face gets redder
the woman from the council
grey/whiter
the Chair just greyer
I slump all adjourn
no lunch we meet on site glances
no time to phone anyone before
the door shifts the angle view of the madman's
house who can give me
something take the edge off endure
suddenly over the threshold of this
house where he died 5 years ago
I am hit by 20 dures years packaged
mad bulls face to paper caricature
for years then Delilah death

while travelling Caution moving conveyer
please take care please hold the handrail
or the numbers of us running how

crept up stole his strength
stand in the booby trap rooms
this man who was mad and violent
measurements are not the same what if the
dure impact suddenly strikes through the
syntagm contiguous time
or the dure is a dead paradigm
my life the interstice erasing time
back back to double negative
present time defeated past
dure elenchus and one more time

Caution moving conveyer please take care
please hold the handrail while travelling
still still hold it mind her foot face oh she

Memo: 'The new girl, the new girl, is steady,
straight and strong,

Gravispace

In the Bag[13]

a number of unknowns power up
despite survival pack
an experienced travelling bag
holds no surprises – go!
I am ready smiling - item:
swiss army knife - for emergencies
painkiller – take me! take me!
tampon - in secret case
book - for public anonymity
ticket - one of several
paper hankies - for sneezing and tears
comb – to be prepared
purse - calculated for need or loss
debit card – might be demands
fastened zip – anti-theft keep out!
screamer - too afraid to use
mobile phone - for love and bonding
plastic bag – to discard
small packet of biscuits – change daily
pen or pencil or both
notebook - new or full/worn
photo or two - motto
'I am a good housekeeper – every

travelling Caution moving conveyer please
take care please hold the handrail while
run for the one with the keys quickly

Memo: 'She knows she has a Union that is helping her along;'

time I get divorced I keep the house'[14]
place - the bag - space - the bonding
time - all day or for weeks on end or
I link the contents of this bag to the bin
frequently and catastrophe strikes
I search everywhere - the back pocket
I can't find keys that control in and out
space marked out by time and
how can I get home tonight without
'MY TICKET! MY PURSE! MY KEYS!'

Getting the Timing Right

I imagine myself to be
then I remember myself
outside the tube station
city life time sliced into three
I am really tired all over the place
I can't find my keys
I re-imagine where are my keys?
I remember where I lost them
fool! fool! losing the plot
gap between sign and signified
I broke the bond with myself
well I bought a new bag changed jobs took
different routes but the bonding
is memory of commuter travel

moving conveyer please take care please hold
the handrail while travelling Caution
just many minutes the paramedic

past this house or that bush or shop
day after day the time alone then and now
the space is made of the same time same place

And it is nothing like

pressure weight of untouchable gravity
slaps real to metaphysical imagine quiet
desire for small breath of wind
in the hot park
soft sound of running water
drinking water
limpid touch of blowing air
sleepless at dawn
breath of perfumed flowers
the smart florists
taste of fresh baked bread all day
pre-baked treat
the sunset over
the flyover warm embrace
welcomes us home
time off with people we love
throws all it has
crashes us in defiant planes

conveyer please take care please hold the
handrail while travelling Caution moving
opens her green bag tries the pulse

Negative Crossings

Interstice One

I have unfinished business
while passing through remember
the river crossing (default)
where debts fall due: it's time time
the ferryman rows and rows
takes his coin in due payment
bears important packages
the documents tell bad news
but this was just the dry run
on a dark November night
when welcomed back echoing
hurrying down passages
flinging open dusty doors
light brought into unswept rooms
giving orders for fires to be lit
the mists rise from the water
there isn't much time then -
in May the blow comes[15] check pack
wait wait till the dawn tide rises
without sleep then leave early
keys as the night clings
to the sodden weeds
dew on thick clothing
door quietly shut

please take care please hold the handrail
while travelling Caution moving conveyer
and watching can you hear me and we

Memo: take 4 stages of examination for W.C.O.'s

final shuffles fears
footsteps pad quickly
down to the mooring
muffled oars swing out
voices muttering
downriver the boat
rocking anchored
tense against the tide
close by Syon turn
our faces seaward
waves scull fears scudding
hopes prove tears
looking back to only the mist
and the past surrendered
unsure of which is closer
quick heartbeat quiet thought
hand of friendship or
fleeting kiss in peace
we did not know that
we plan ahead and
include that chance of/
and maybe never

Interstice Two

home from a weekend away
to find that burglars have been

hold the handrail while travelling Caution
moving conveyer please take care please
repeating ***the time words occupy***

push wide the unlocked door
drawers open tell secrets
dusty leaves on the bare floor
the caption of expletives
raw feelings bereavement rage
intakes is that gone and this?
the back door hanging by hinges
letting in the time to come
and letting out time before
I am swept back to the river
where pleasure boats dip jostle
back by the water with mists
rolling in on the evening
the ferryman smoothly pulls his oars
back and forth 'that ferryman
should get an outboard motor!'
not recognising that time
overlays clear images
with dark moments as payment
for services rendered
there is a fight going on
he has strong hands stomach heart
that she might bend like a willow
but will not snap has life warm hands
her heart is in it she does not fall
even when she sees her own blood
up against the wall
down on the ground and

handrail while travelling Caution moving
conveyer please take care please hold the
in recitation – consists of so

hitting the pavement
hard against hubris
I knock sharp against bricks and bins
my eyes have been taken out by
darkness and illumined by light
the protective layers stripped
the light grows dark and uncharted
the air the breath
the smell of the river
there was no deed for surrender
no official record
(but some books were already gone)[16]

Interstice Three

whose war is it anyway against whom and
how often does insurgency hit home it's more
like Beirut who monopolises these words?
I can see the signs of unrest
battering and harm unleashing cries
'I just wanted to touch them'[17]
breaking my heart and yours
the river flows comfortless
each glister of sweat in sunlight
a moment in history and see the signs?
lyric poetry is the greatest
embellishment'[18]
notebook in hand he has set the mike

hold the handrail while travelling Caution
moving conveyer please take care please
many lines – the syllable is long

have you hit fundamental?
who has the right to ask questions?
would I tell you if I knew?
what is a passion?
we have time for more questions
in the silence there is time
which is given space
the signs are that the foundations have
shifted made a nexus innocence
reset with the purpose (defaulting)
unnoticed you pursued your own ends
such simple tactics so effective
for promotion optics ravelling
masked codes through zones of
                                        voice degrees
articulation in wastes (reset
default) of diffidence the passion
still seems felt - we see your display or
we could use delay design new signs

Interstice Four

to carry this truth down the years
to bear defeat and shoulder time
weld memory to wrought iron
gates through which we may not pass
the tale is simply retold
we need no grindings of will

travelling Caution moving conveyer please
take care please hold the handrail while
        for it is double the length of a short one

odes triumphant eulogies
no well trodden rehashes
scatterings of gold pavings
the air grows dark (and cheap)
'The man who laughs has simply not
yet had the terrible news'[19]
I can tell this isn't the sort of joke
you feel inclined to laugh at
the ferryman breathes in time to his
sculls
we have gone and returned gone again
in terror irreversible distress
who he was, what we saw and did with that
heavy load indeterminate wrapped
in folds and folds
around a bloodied stone
carrying more than our bodies weight
suffering unfinished business of a
different kind that follows on the heels
of time crossings (default) passing

Caution moving conveyer please take care
please hold the handrail while travelling
for the lines are long – do we

Memo: 'To use an 'Underwood' is to realise how
fascinating typing may become'

Collective Stare

my voice disappeared when
my throat dried up with
witness the audience rouse to
let us we beg you we
present our requests here
discarding of jackets
rustling of papers
all eyes turn to
the result of deeds not
the content first arrests
the attention of passers-by
who look at the people with
voices stand aside let them
filtering though ranks they come
jostled impeded jeered at
the rulers make themselves
invisible day and night
as security guards or
dressed in gowns and wigs or
robes white coats masks oh
I invite judgment or
allocate prophecy or
exhort reward or
provide response to
slip out any time to

please take care please hold the handrail while
travelling Caution moving conveyer
use a shorter time to measure a

talk to strangers who
evoke no fear only
future time let live here
leave me to unravel freely out of
a single statement made by
your working conditions about
disaffection punishment or
knowledge reflective as
time write a letter of
protest I will take to
the streets without
my interface between
words said to be said
feelings I have leave to
your mythology or to
the political rostrum to
as a matter of fact this
poet's voice takes over
from the personal breathe
substitute voice we
argue we like the noises
blood to my face of
adrenalin my shaking
hands have their
place in compatible
words and poet
and rhapsody[20]

conveyer please take care please hold the handrail while travelling Caution moving
her face is dull white we turn glancing

Arches[21]
To B C

some kind of
and there
from within and without
I walk in shaded triangles
and into light
(I think this is a God given place)
and palaver and paloma
and imprint
turning
just to see the shadows
of arches shifting
I walk past pillars

something
and that
above and below
I am shaded haptic
into past
(I think this is a God given place)
and maelstrom and mayhem
and breath
living
in time to see the light
of arches shifting
I walk under arches

please take care please hold the handrail while travelling Caution moving conveyer
measuring a not knowing hope or

Memo: Mr Eliot can you calculate our annual leave?[22]

somewhere
and this
beside and within
I am light chiralled
and swept
(I think this is a God given place)
and is and is not is
and glints
throwing
off the sunbaked air
of time shifting
I walk past roses

and some
and those
around and outer
I walk through scents
and then dark
(I think this is a God given place)
and ease and embrace
and touchstone
walking
towards home
into darkness shifting
I walk past pillars

care please hold the handrail while travelling
Caution moving conveyer please take
within itself takes twice as long

Memo: as we are gravely underpaid

some errors
and these
under and beneath
albescent and umbrescent
and tear touched
(I think this is a God given place)
and torment and adamantine
and face up
laying
from radiant tombstone
how does she
I walk past grace

and shadows…

**hold the handrail while travelling Caution
moving conveyer please take care please**
please use the lift

DEATH

Starless Night

Looking outward on a starless night
chased stars have stolen away in fright
then inward, when thieving gorging light
remorseless turns Iris' wheel of sight,
casts future fortune asunder blight, white.

What might happen next with dread or so
the thinking goes where despair meets hope
and blundering earthquakes of body and soul
portend through rabid faults that woe on woe
leak through, interrupt flow – know with no.

Supplanting glimmer glisten with black
and the task before me lack and lack
ashes shift cradle sprung year's last spark
not generating more, dying back
for longer than life then black and dark.

Dead light[23] is all chimaeras, seers, fears,
emetic, uses cathartic tears,
is bleak, attacking weak seismic sere
blotting deadening build up of arrears
just one physical movement turns years.

Change reject to rejection - cast, strike
adapt to adaptation – this might
let bruised life take charge – effort flight
choreograph bright light – flash of sight
nought to some cognition in the night.

Seven Seven[24]

then it rained
hey says a stranger passing
drizzle steady hard
there's no buses since two and won't be 'til six
smells turn from damp to wet
where are they? I think yes it's quiet
fresh fresh green and a hint of London rose
I check – it's 3.30
pleasure sharp rises in the mid afternoon
why I say what's the matter
haven't you heard about the bombs?
green ran dark under a passing cloud
dark green and darker shadow conceals
decisive
I think - I didn't hear any bombs
colour deepening shade
they've bombed the tube they think seven dead
this could be red on red
a well of anger rises in me
turning to darker brown
one for which I cannot shut off the light
what's that smell?
I shout when? where?
when does rose turn red
Kings Cross central London and on a bus
I think of dark red blood red
how far away is the sky
or hope or future or finality
light shades darken here
I think of yellow
it's gone very quiet
they could pick on buildings instead

I watch an extra scattering of walkers
who are directly concerned with tactics and
strategies
Oh you're home!
lists names
who is not coming home tonight?
they said to go home at 3 and I've walked
the hot day draws closer to evening and
nightfall
you are surprisingly on top of things after all
that
darkness steals towards my shadow
how far how long?
dusk leaches the colours
well it's half past 5 now -2 ½ hours
there is no yellow here
and it's not a bad walk - through Hampstead
dark suffusion carmine shaded with black
not in these shoes of course
I wince from desperate cries
I look down and blank out
and silence that betokens ends
a flashback of lit entombment
voices with the strength shattered out
40 minutes longer in the tunnel waiting
darkening tones descending to whimpers
I had the day off today
I'll be a real stickler for bags and parcels now
make a real lemon of myself I don't care
when the lights go out what colour is life then?
Tonight we have to drive home
we turn the car radio on and listen
it's quiet
for a moment it's great without the traffic

there's silence
scared we drive through Neasden Stonebridge
Park
down to Acton Vale speed unimpeded by
articulated buses
jerking with hostility through Victorian high
streets
empty roads empty pavements
no one is home yet or out yet
what is the colour of defeat?
meshed with powerlessness
eaten into by incomprehension
by conserving rage get through the day
opening into night
now the lights are on
I wake at 5.30 a.m. and see the night buses
black women go to work past Shepherd's Bush
have I the right to sleep?
they are impassive and stare straight ahead
sleepy worried in the early morning light
darkness into day
impassioned only within
the colour of sadness concealing
shadow by brightening light
dignity behind you back lit
do they belong in the half light
and get on with the day
and what is the colour....
dark red?
who wears the black cap
cardinal heart pivot
write in red
reprieve reprisal

stay of execution lose your chance
eleventh hour last thing
cold storage in the hold up working in
the very high temperatures hell on earth
clearing up
this is a debit that I did not personally pay
but pay for
in arrears to a pound of flesh and rising
the sum is now greater than the spectrum
allows
overdrawn in the red or pay on delivery
live on credit what is the colour of isolation
the colour of disconnection
the colour of asymmetry
that you were there and I was here
unclassified parentheses
temperature rising
rootless colours insular
disproportionate amongst the pale tired faces
it's all off-target off-centre episodic
what is the colour of episodicity
the colour of sharp carmine vermilion
extraneous colours on a hot summer's day
you got home yesterday now travelling
shades are hallowed hailed
read as times these times in tunnels
we are not all present
the sound of the bell is red
the light of the tunnel is white
the colour of raw flesh is livid
the tone of the heart is dark

Mirror Neuron[25]

One plus One

sit with me in a bay window seat
while we recall your bittersweet love
of the friend who passes through your life
giving no reason to stay just one
quiet moment giving one to one
who lost her mother as a child this
reason I want our friendship to last
who nods agreement with me when
you are delighted with your present
your moment of warm surprise a charm
moving express anticipation
discover surprise delight pleasure
is she going to thank me she does
warm sunshine spreads fingers across backs
flows glowing from polished wooden floor
to our wood carved seat can anyone
doubt that pleasure is passing reason
not arising from despair no reason
pleasure through lit galleries surely

uncertain reflection do you find
this hard to deal with and each other
shall we discuss the exhibits then
gain our affection through empathy
is this a reason can anyone doubt
our interest reciprocation?
I interpret the silences between
us and exhibit one - young woman
with dyed red hair - mask of silence sees
statue - Sorrow with a marble veil

is this a reason for atrophy
immovable grief in cast marble
face carved out set by human force
we neither have money for coffee
reason to buy one postcard instead
saying you have your reasons leaving
coldness in the vast entrance goodbye
we say I run upstairs mirrored
steps in once seen musty galleries
then reason warmed by exercise
cold to warm to static exhibits
cluttered, spaced, opening out
vistas step back close in peer pass by
there is Sorrow again her face set
just glancing through her marble veil at -
she's gone - I look back down marble stairs -
the opiate sumptuousness rich
plethora of colour emotion
ravished by emotional excess -
intellect lifts Sorrow's carvèd veil?
she stares forever through the window
where we sat and I have a postcard

Equals Two

jumping up from her seat after tea
she ran to the board started scribbling
laughing impossible names writing
flight delight squeak pun after pun flew
from her chalk excited being a child
I watched mesmerised I said - you
are laughing all the time you write and
underneath the nervous temper could
fly out at any time words spring out

in juxtaposition overlay
mirror receiving the wit her gift
comes upon parts of stasis move me
family trees glitter pedigrees
arise from the top of the board down
spread tickles in buttery sunlight
I laughed until my sides hurt and she
laughed at me took pleasure in her jokes
I must copy it down said save it
and make a difference for ever
'til Sorrow lifted her face, as yet
still veiled - turn about face to true
face veiled sorrow but why do this
and the other truth the others not
understanding a secret life born
here in words posit the difference
everyone surprised what is this
how she went back the next morning and
added to it for a week worked
ideas through the generations
together with her laughter and how
I ran to see each morning what else
was new - write some more please do more
she smiled and said she might she might
and didn't I lovingly read out names
echoed the laughter with smiles please turn
your head to look 'But death with ruthless
hand on golden haire'[26] a long time passed
'til never 'Black , and in black, a woman
did appeere, Furie with hir, such as
I scarcely knowe' attenuated
last memory

Blue Plaque

we meet - lunch at 12 - she has cancer
she is losing weight the hourglass tells
she has a new wig like a film star
tends to crash out a falling meteor
her husband who is lost without her
faithful servant who waits tirelessly
even if the orders do not come
pinning future hope on her new dog
limpet to territory of hope
bright with effort thin sun breaking out
thoughtlessly on a cool summer's day
she is devastated by illness
a politician rounded on by
a significant misdemeanour
time's dial indicators elided
each night then day turns time around

Bound[27]

Waxwork of the streets a shaking frame
hesitant amid the traffic flow
meandering amongst hoots
and reeling in cold morning air
coughing sputum on the tarmac
blood flecked?   chance

hand wave to the sky prima balance
careening in slow motion
patterns of petals leaves dying
the drivers roar past then a hearse
on both sides herald of passage
a few flowers   'God…'

and the change from imprecation to
invocation the getting out
and how coldness skewed sticks
fever without recompense pays
entangled in space logic time
placed here   stet

slowing his swaddling bands unwinding
hesitant bounds and points and dance
thoughts heart's eyes pavement to kerb
dervish undone dancing ribbons
destination collapsing from
just moving   who

Cause and Effect

Now my boss is pregnant and while
she is on maternity leave
I have to do her work for her
but I have no clearance powers
no status no extra bonus.

I ring her up each morning 'Hi'
how *are* you and the little one
to be?' shall I send this, reject
that, forward this, but your process
of selection causes me trouble.

Each time the management ask for
reports up-dates you write yourself
personally you delay the
inter-department paperwork -
I want to take over your job.

But I think you will be back when
the little emperor is born
I try to avoid phoning you
so you phone me up again say
'why you don't phone what's happening'.

I worry about Zara in
the next office muscling in on
I try to keep it secret hide
this telling off 'I really want
your suggestions' mumbling I
want to be promoted not her

I walk for miles from Victoria to Euston
my mother does not eat since the operation
she thought nothing of it arriving with a bag
holding papers anxiety blocking sunshine
passing through customs wanting to succeed
through rooms to a council flat treated to death
in the home of the young breadwinner
how does the *rite de passage* go…?
Work for years for shit wages
then you're entitled to the same
the lines are down
don't ask me where I'm from I'm just black
there is an interruption the LED
shows two headlines at once glare from broken
neon pulses of light in time to irritate
just before the alarm is raised that's for you

Impact

pressure gauge rises and falls
accept the beating traffic thundering
the speed of travel
hitting the destination with force
let me tell you where you are
the buildings weep asbestos tears
reworked by the survivor
the end of the story is guessed at
bustling at 19 across cleaned floors
laying out 5 casualties in a night
an uneasy torpor in supervised rooms
iron grip self-discipline
the hindsight more than she can bear
she did not mind at the time

reaching out to touch the victims[28]
the injuries were horrific
she gave her time without pay
to stare hell in the face
and face it down
personal pain forced into heroism
blood and time reel in backwards
the colours are filtered
red filter plus time redder

the survivor checks on everyone
this one needs tucking up
here fresh saline
watch the temperature on this one
here there are clusters
machine checked
one lies cocooned pale unresponsive
distress report
we have investigated monitored
established…
taken him down to theatre
brought him up to the ward
drug after monitor and drug
this memory cloak is intact
cold outside here in the warm
looks bleak a vista of calamity

Force

Aim:
Is it wiser to undo the code find where rationality defeats 'emotions that reinforce confirmation bias'[29]

Method:
'disconfirm' the sense of the expected that
stasis moves in an orderly fashion hold keys to
ratios and probabilities holds movement within
itself confers owner stability hears the ticking
stops sees turned faces registering unexpected
hiatus through uncertainty

Experiment:
my face has fallen   my heart has stopped
as everything crashes   serotonin uptake rushes
at breakneck speed the survivor is also affected
the politicians are ready
'reinterpret disconfirmatory evidence'
'our conclusions feed happy lies into news
                                                  machines'
take the voices that shout clearest and loudest
peripheral chipping away by concision
pinched with tiredness after a 12 hour shift

Result:
she wrapped her cloak around her after
unbelieving staring at the figures
in the blood rush the statistics broke down
maybe you trade on disjunction
dislocation abandoning the cloaks
for jackets which provide less warmth
in the early hours I heard his last words
not recorded and they confirm nothing

Conclusion:
count the minor details of the one who saw
motive on the face of the dead man tearing a
strip off calling a spade shouting over the

speaker cut all short making all the listeners
shake in their shoes the door rattle with the
shouting rapid eye movements largely the
hearts freeze the breath stops and this
one and this one start to cry and that one and
that one retreat muttering into their shells these
ones individually say we never heard there
was a problem and these ones who have
already left say that they did not believe that
there was anything worth saying or hearing
and nothing wrong gabbling way out this way

Report:
when leaden eyed in afternoon hours
the light buzzes off/on and the lamp glares
ever larger as the focus grows dim
I dream of beds or sofas to lie down
the buzzing glow gets hold of me
I accentuate moment and sound but
heavy lids close someone passes fresh files
open a new folder name with endnotes
the wind gets up the door bangs in seconds
the papers fly up scatter the light is
bright is is is is again drink water
mark a unit of time stretch don't ask me
which one it was interlude to compress
information your database to mine
think that's half the job done and half of it
this half and half that again and again
just a cough nothing just play with the pause
between breaths wooden headed inclined
to doze the light breaks through the dreams
sparking tears from driving so hard upon
the stones[30]

The Poet is Dead

Triumphed over by death herself
who mourns this death but other poets?
together now 'Everything new
is better than everything old'[31]
the funeral is at Mortlake Crem.
at noon prompt for the muse, publisher,
solicitor, family, close friends
and tenebrous Fame attends in time
treading on the wreaths in her haste
'I would rather have had the money'
she spits finding the will is clearly
correct rather than advantageous

'what is there to mourn if the words are there?'
the publisher bristles self important
'I have here a copy of her last poems'
the literary executor puffs and
shuffles papers 'I'll take a cut on that'
the muse impatient shifts her fluid gaze
from poet's photo to anthologies
prompting her friend (with paper hanky) says
'it's a sad business losing her in
this way the poem only half written
what of dramatic integrity or
a proper suspension of disbelief
she's gone so suddenly can we only get to the
bottom of this by studying her intended
breathing I thought I heard her voice
quite clearly as I read page 76'

this death was really not intended
the artic[32] misjudging at traffic lights

it was quite obvious said the witness
that the driver would have seen her clearly[33]
demonstrating the events again with
true words acting imitating details
derived (see poet commissioned
by point of view) allows conclusions drawn
what she did not write or live for/die of

the literary executor tucks
the unauthenticated drafts under
his arm says 'I'll collect the urn later'
turning to leave - the next cortège purrs in
family and friends are not hard headed
succumb to emotion in a hotel
with a single drink and a small sandwich
construct interest in a public reading
between the lines no distance how her life!
'what a lifelike portrayal!'[34] illusion
engendered by errors in this text
perhaps without accepting experience
the publisher's responsibility
'what you are seeing now is a repeat.'[35]

the poet plays mind games on her harp
the painted setting seems idle enough
but too misty and without much colour
is there an impassioned re-vision of
Dante-esque proportions suppliant words
plangent yearning bathos just hanging there
memories swiftly falling from hearing
in harmony with the air we breathe
unseen fulcrum unknown focus only
unattended I would like to think that
the mockery is light hearted poet speaks

words fall unheard from tongue to page
and taking out the silence from the stage
why take the trouble to honour intent?
when all was taken down a path as meant
I would not calmly open up old wounds
I cannot tackle the tasks as simply sounds
here is deep intention profoundly found
cast in bricks cement and in one bond bound
hinges glass panes metaphors simile
where to next my friend? you have yet to see
start out think back and forth you need to
know
what the reader says the answers come go
we take our numbered points in good part
know 'from' and 'belonging' right from the
start[36]

bye baby bystander
over overall hover
upheaval upper uppity
attack attitude atrophy
next nix nexus
thunder under blunder
lit. ed. despairs 'this is no use to me'
project shelved papers filed bib. cut
index amended contents forgotten
'Look out!'
abandon conscious separation
the poet's story effects direct
changeover - a new contract! –
presents comment with narrator
explains the word and word and epic reader
(with chorus)[37]

Predatory Oration[38]

Take 1

today it's a fat politician
that eats everything/everyone
falling asleep afterwards with the
confidence of a child in public
now for what is about to happen
can I move through this terrain safely
regulations answer it is safe
as such I never travel alone

and the questions are not my friends
I can state without confidence
circumstances frame this approach
the storm is getting closer and
leaves rustle outside the window
the effect is astonishing
I thought I was settling at last
but extra fright sends me backwards

→ get mugged by a man with a hammer[39]
→ try to seize hammer and push man away
→ lose voice through fear, cannot even scream
→ neighbour calls police
→ neighbour tells intruder to leave
→ outnumbering brings results
→ police are not sympathetic tell me to leave
the area
→ neighbour glares at me for causing trouble!
→ I thank neighbour for potentially saving my
life
→ I do not know his name
→ he moves and I do not see him again

→ spend several weeks:
← dreaming about men with hammers or other implements
← waking in distress suddenly in the night
← looking for self defence classes to go to - all too expensive
←taking books out of the library
←study line drawings of how to defeat the assailant
← try out the movements with a friend
←she hates doing it - it's no use
← buy shoes without heels so I can run faster
← give up wearing skirts
← realise that there is no consolation prize
← no sure way
← that someone may strike again sometime soon
← get used to the idea
← hope it doesn't happen again

Take 2

female smaller than me
money/knife
victim/living survivor
alive/woman *in the city*
fear *city*/emotional dynamic
work train to the city hive
oh in the *city*
here in the *city*
going up to *London*
not seismic or attributes
prime minister's question time/
the council estate
dying alone/
and the riches
we see this part close up

I see you sitting in front of the tv /
and comprehend the gridlock
I am endlessly deadening
down for a final answer
to ratify dreams pinned against

Take 3

let's sit down to lunch what would you like?
time and this conversation unfolds
the afternoon is almost over
the photo shows men sitting at table
a picture of the elected shows
Leigh Pemberton and Thatcher sitting down to
lunch at Downing Street
that means he must have the job:
fact: this one meal (watch carefully) means
you'll live to fight another day
survive the bastards and drama -
made redundant without warning
or your son was caught with a class one drug
fact: the utter relief of
not giving this meal a second thought
proves we can give slow death a chance

Pan out

the metonymic city we most long to forget
events and excitement survive away from danger
the most intense effects let me break the routine
save up for the holiday I breathe heavily
go another plus minus defeat all over again
disconfirm life gritty in the confines of a city
overall explicitly dust metonymicity

Peroration by Punctuation

,breathe in breathe out, breathe in,...[40]
rhetorical purpose greyed out
,there is always an afterwards
,any peroration simply...
this body language is worth more
,than a kineme or two[41] but - I
read him like an open book after
, - we – ,the dots prefer dashes...
them - but the conclusion is always...
it hardly serves, the end when it comes
,I have yet to be persuaded
,combinations are persuasive

concludes...

FAME

Dull

liars who lay the word to rest in recognition of
and the next silence comes after the report direct from
voices over-ride still in time finished letter envelope forfeit this
noise directed to hums rumbles intimate enhance footsteps given
open shut fix points speak maximum clarity through backgroun
voices coming going driven like so far sound waves doors bang
oiled primed mind recognition resolution this is it melding the
dull the book of Fame sounds as it falls to the faultline

SHOUT! SHOO! OUT! SHUT! SHOUT!!

hirsute and
nipping claws
heaving eating
termagent termagent
scything tossed
arrant mites
fulminous over
rough dregs
nice
stropp ergonomics
in numbers
bearing down
born borne
to smithereens
coming at us
caissonous teeth

nice

midden happy
crawing claws
music in their ears
terror pinches
how they drone
how they fly
how they come
nice
for the crumbs
hoping hopping
landing eating
strike once
and once past
not enough
not enough
noise ose ise
noise ose ise
nice one nice
nice one nice
903513
315309
POESIE
EISEOP

POESIE

Ms Pixel Writes:

‘searching……’
the bricks or building blocks
construct the city
not only is there no vantage point
there is only the other
out there
we are the alienated moving
parts cemented into time

If pixelated
person without memory
constructed
responsive through lighting up
now

‘I am Ms Pixel’
‘Cute name I like that’
‘I have been born without a memory
but I have recognition
I am here to tell you
“There’s Something About Mary”
(insert post code and swipe card)

uddenly remember that Ms Pixel is
in colour
I turn her off too and look around
the now dark room.

‘Death triumphs over the poet
but what about the dark?’
Mary can be heard laughing
triumphant warm and
welcoming deep in
e darkened room contains no dust
the hands of the clock are indistinct
osing in allows inner crosscurrents
nock against the panes of the soul
only the black and shadow
not the journey to the unknown
washed in sunset light reflected
from glass cold skyscrapers
directly into the rear view mirror
and back into my eyes
I am clothed in sunset.

Mary stares at the ceiling

the experiment is the establishment
of a black and white reality in legals.
Romeo and Juliet type -
that's all she sees'

'She lives in a shuttered room
with only her computer
for company in black and white
we are proving there is no innate
perception.
What does Mary know?'

Mary knows more than she lets on
reticent undisturbed
when the bell rings it is time for supper
we may watch Mary eat.
On Mondays she has human contact.'
I look at my watch - it is midnight now
on Friday -
I turn Mary off.

'Can she see colour?'
We are always being asked that'
says Ms Pixel with a winning smile.

''She remains here until
have the results in black and white'
Ms Pixel does not smile
'our ambition is to see the results
with references
She does not understand colour
she has never seen it.
We will make money from her.
We will show her photos in 2025 and
ask her to identify the colours.'

'I have to rescue Mary'
Is she pixelated too
and I by transference -
watching without interpretation?
Is this ambitious of me?
Can I get killed for this?
Am I responsible here
for *demise en scene*
we are watching a little death in parts
I must get to her before...
capture an essence of at least
without escaping from the unseen

ambition of the experimenters.
Go past the dragons!
The point of conclusion is other than
describing recursive sunset.

She does not know about virtual res
battleship pixels in process
at the M25 near Potters Bar
shall I meet the lovely Ms Pixel?
Let's have fluffy stories amongst the
meaty ones -
but is Ms Mary pixelated too
or do I believe it all
time yes place no
space has the ambitions -
See the light! See the light!
between the spotlights
I cut the chainlink fence.
Security is poor
investment levels are low
the spectator's ambition is vicarious
enjoy! enjoy!

'you know,
we have a place for you here.'
Symmetry through compilation
timeless pixelation
she looks so right
right to the heart of me I know
she's there for me.
Ms Pixel does not reply
it's just an appearance you know

Mary will now sleep
Ms Pixel is on standby

ness is haloed by the outsides arcs
white spots and flares
lights swing past the windowspan
light and dark
now and there
here and then
place plus time: place times time

Headlines;
Black and White
Escapes in the Night

trap the alarm into silence
with an electro magnetic barrier ke
adjusting to the dark red glow
of the fire alarms back up generator
lights I try doors -
peer down staircases -
there is no imminent sense of release.
Suddenly Ms Pixel is there beside me
'I know what you're looking for'
she said
her voice is soft and low
'Who'
'No, what' she said
Now I must escape by the skin of my
real teeth engage in episodic challeng
reality is not where the best abstracts
really are.
It's no use', she said softly.
I have always had this ambition
to speak with such modulated
soft vowels with no glottal front edge
controlled entirely by a technologicall
perfect diaphragm.
Ms Pixel looks at me admiringly

Philosophers do not hang back:
'We have been discussing this for years'

In the post two days later
there is a letter from Mary

"I have dictated this letter to Ms Pixel.
I know what they are trying to do.
It has been explained to me many times.
But I don't have much time
and born in the wrong place
just this space - oh justly put -
Red is the colour of sunset
Brown is the colour of my hair
Green is the colour of my eyes
and the windows are clear
Ms Pixel is devoted to their entertainment.
She promises this letter will reach you
that there is just time.
To begin with they would not let me read
I do not know how long
there is unjust time

colour does not need to be proved
only interpreted
there is a just place
to reveal the calculations
their proof of one through
opposition to another will demonstrat
here is an unjust place
just space
I can live with brown and black and
I can prove what they wanted to know
(unless of course they are colour blin
there is unjust space
I have enjoyed the reading
Ms Pixel says I have read virtually al
books in the experimental station libr
and she can always get me more
I am running out of space.....
remember pity is locked
the files are copied
I have the code and will be back
N5N5S6S

I dial up Ms Pixel

this number does not receive inco
calls....this number does not recei

There's Something About Mary
2004
Peter Ludlow , Yujin Nagasawa
and Daniel Stoljar (Eds.)
Cambridge MA
MIT Press

er streets shift dust gathers vision scars so far so stasis rules

sions to watch....

in our jail 150 people killed

hazard large enough

world cup'

different place later wastes familiar slight

ssing the thames estuary

not built up yet

all is well appropriate hub

keep tabs in a

clean fresh

asis levels are low fearful of

general way

exploding boat docks

want fresh food.

M25 Clockwise

the luminous carapace defies the
serried stygian giants
cradling the has and is
and 'is' the greater force against
ranks with throttles harnessed
feet poised as spurs *terse roar*
hurried whip hand
commanding stasis if not peace
asymmetric cloaks of fumes
resolute in lines
eight lane gyrus
vibrations too hard to bear *dread nurse*
translucent grafting of hand to head
mother's hand round fontanelle
face white with shock standing
by car with crippled wing
bonded to rear wheels
felled broken shells *first glance*
mobilised by arms and desperate need
shouts unheard beneath engines
faces turned to judge the crucial run
mother as moment eye judges the line
father's hands with child in each
rushing from reservation to shoulder
wince freeze

axles knuckled down
whipped terror wedged
a blinding roaring pulsion
blink I'm gone anticlockwise
the miracle is the not bleeding
brief humanity the will be *ease tense*

Slurp.exe[42]

my eyepods grow heavy
slurping belly pendant
grunting falling dead weight
round the park lizard like
with half shut eyes staring
a tale of events that
patter after chatter
dragging backwards in time
slip a haze between me
and them leaden lazy
in the heat. I sit down
on the bench and with a -
give a massive belch so
people gasp turn their heads
I slurped at the spent
fountain of knowledge 'til
broken it doesn't work
children still run around
the dry basin crying
hissst I have slurped up
politicians and bombs
debates and rhetoric
tactics and the language
survives excuse me
are you still there? Pointless
I phone Time how are you
are you OK - silence
well yeah I've never run
so fast before I feel
strange and different I
get away quickly
sipped exe-slurping

filed on flecks of chip
then forgotten which name
which... the presenter looks
as if he’s had only
a few hours sleep - that's new
didn't I tell you that
the .exe chip brought back
memories induced
haze of undigested -
the phone - Aristotle
Hi - do you peddle truth
narration then proof[43]
soles of lead truth limping
before focus on the
speaker *himself*? Did it
really happen so quick
there was real running
and what I chose
to tell you: not 'I have
spoken, you have heard, you
have the facts, [I am] judge'[44]
shades of truth intervene
that's not what I recall
did you get on alright
were you nervous today
I counted 35
all armed police in
the space of 10 minutes
I've never felt so safe
meagre truth clothed in
complex hue and hissing
touching sensations now
rarely available

£50.00 cash[45]

peel away the layers
street furniture cars
parked
bus powering through
with inches to spare
behind the stand by the
racks
in the clothes
department
the tired 50+ woman
buying a blouse for
£50.00 cash
she has been working
all night
needs a bath
dull eyes defensive
prostitute at 9.30am
my fingers grow tired
typing out the words:
'I wish she had slept
well'
how do you know she
wasn't *safe*
from disease,
aggression,
objectification
she works when *he* says
so
and gives him his large
cut
the tariff for tonight's
hard tumescent passion

I pick up the tube/bus
map at the newsagent
accept the dirt and dust
do not inhale deeply
spring back/aside if
someone gets close
manoeuvre the best
place
get on the train first
avoid eye contact
with changing
individuals:
the art of ratcheting
torment in 10 easy
steps:
1. keep the woman up
all night demanding
sex or food hit her

rides
working prolapsed or
childless
this is a street with
shops and
I cannot change that
no give
what do you expect
up against thrown up
against
spliced between the
grey flags
I get very emotional
about work
the manager the
customer
and splitting head
tiredness
time off promotion
spokes
winched around the
hub

2. constantly change
your mind as to what
you want and how you
want it hit her
3. make your own
arrangements for
leisure and just say 'I'm
going out now' hit her
4. say you haven't got
your pay this week so
there's nothing for food
hit her
5. say you're not
hungry at the last
minute as the food is
ready and go out hit
her before you go
6. bring a friend round,
whisper and laugh and
drink hit her
7. buy a new expensive
personal item – camera,
suit – something nice
for yourself – use it in
her face hit her
8. shout 'I don't know
what you're talking
about' when watching
TV hit her
9. say 'no woman
drives *my* car' hit her
10. promise to take her
out and hit her[46]

hope is an engineer
attend to the levels -
nuts and bolts city –
buildings triumph over
city routines
power bases triumph
over buildings
the forces of greed
triumph over
powerbases
an individual walks
away bankrupt
triumphant
over the insurance
market
if they have left us any
money to pay for it
the buildings the job
loneliness sights
crowds money endless
poor quality cheap
food
shabby grubby
endlessly
in the crowds on a hot
sunny day
one free space on the
park bench
the stray dog cocks his
leg on whoever sits
there
the grass is hot grey
litter strewn
sit silent among words

from a friend with bad
                    nerves
I only get 30 mins for
                    lunch
if I screw this -

and back again to hope

Vantage

old bricks worn air
worms
round old corners
falls
down staircase wells
speaks
ghosts of voices
hang
still in the dank air
scuffs
dust corners with dull bulbs the child
swings
on the stair secrets and memories
creep
impersonally through time
dredges
happiness now
lapses
in through the back window quick
remove
forgotten toys
crying through the night
start
nothing is the ending
take
the unhappy child
opens
the door undressed in
ruins
the wall paint
peels off

the roar at the end of the road
reruns
sad Greek neighbours
watch
thinking of dry mountainsides
lift
thick grey air rising up
sublimate
smells the wind
breathe
yesterday
hits
home the weekend dust
races
this weekend
masks
a careful city system
erodes
eternity
defused
the furniture
stays
exactly the same why
say
you always have a home here
even the photos
give
nothing away

Home! home! chair! chair! grapes! grapes![47]

suddenly you say sitting down
about your son with asperger's
suddenly saying sitting down
about your son with asperger's
I looked up as you came in
you sat down and suddenly said
'my son has asperger's'
between thin slices of empathy
lie slivers of truth that disappear
as soon as we focus on them I
do not interrupt to ask "'what makes
a verbal message a work of art?'"[48]

later I arrive note the date awake
memory understand part (on the whole)[49]
again dates arriving here now so soon
memory awakens here and now all
over again my eyes meet your eyes held
unexpectedly on a hot tube train
skeleton framework moments on the grid
of hours tunnel and vertebrae rushing
through hot air carriage following carriage

the quality of the source materials
is vital statistics reveal how close
to the surface the cord lies quantum slips
measurement between hot bodies - 2 cms
two travelling objects crammed *speeding*
stationary same carriage referent
to referent in time though
allowing for the slippage carefully
not touching reshuffling of positions

the extra relief after Camden Town

I bang the door bin men slam shout 'we don't
take these'
closed window polythene draft cold excluder
really blue walls damp damage stains sick
friend next door
meniscus city pure translucent fatty globules
rising rising viscosity surface tension
support the weight? yes! two! one! count there
is a fourth[50]
why Turgenev goes to a club smart orator
radish pumpkin mare turnip peasant woman
kasha kasha[51] persistently travel to work
frame smile look sharp for God's sake if only
the bonus
will pay for a new washing machine

harness forces necessity
home ticket key heating talk
bed heat flushes corners opens
wounds closing doors day off time
sit sit comfort comfort[52] line by
line double lock the front door
checking the time walking away
nothing as always as meaning
nothing much[53] suddenly say
recall again again me you
this that gelling the city
the firm distance between us is
tremendous and very dull
hazy dust movement dust that hangs
I say 'home! home! chair! chair! grapes! grapes!'

Fulcrum at work

Equilibrium

balance off balance corridors and rooms
and rooms and rooms sounds and clatters
                                        bangs thuds
drawers open close someone stretches arms
raised in the swivel chair flex knee back
I meet you at the water dispenser
'Oh how are you getting on - seen *him* yet?'
'taking a break?' 'oh holiday where? when?'
is her pock marked face a barrier
to happiness but the lazy voice speaks -
after the time lapse - before she answers
anything that's put to her I wonder
if she really hears or whether she needs
that moment to ward off danger before
she replies balancing black against white
anyway it's too hot at the wellhead
there's no point in complaining of pressure
each coffee break the line manager sits
at the top of the fire escape with the
new young secretary right next to him
I would rather not be her as there are
other patterns adjust strike the balance
I move my chair and by looking towards
the window onto a brick wall reassess
my position this is not the right file
the smiles are uniform questions routine
everyday everyday mentor
clock voracious time ticks guzzling efforts
yawning people going sounds emptying
lights turned off and silence increasing

then here is the cleaner he stands holding
the polisher in the doorway his smile
has come from equatorial desert
I do not ask him where he is from and
I think of him in one room or with friends
or girlfriend periphery mystery
he is much darker more recent than me
I say 'It's ok I'm finished now'
he balances on his machine and smiles
and smiles 'you go ahead' I say - he will
the clock flashes the seconds just the same

Substitution balance

another artic shudders by three cars
silencing the noise of my bus step up
I am part of the lion's roar sitting
in the belly of this wild animal
carrying me home panther like it leaps
on through ranges of diesel adjustments
gearing up and fine tuning its inbuilt
balancing mechanisms veering to stop
pressing itself close to the scratching post
snapping doors open past the uvula
which hardly moves as the oysters file past
do you go as far as the Elephant?
the passenger error risks eviction
sands flow nods crisis past not looking
swipe the card he suddenly hey hey! hey!
someone turns the column of food stops dead
as a small adjustment in the bite size
takes place you didn't swipe your card beep
beep the cry of oysters the lurching power
driven begins and hassles and hastens

with the staring morsels counting down stops
I read the paper but not much
she reads a novel relentless
he stares ahead into a file
lying unopened in his brain
children laze about and mutter
and squirm and snatch and pull
the LED is a giveaway every
bus arrives in seven minutes
waiting REM sleep balances on the
cusp of waking Frozen Eye Glaze

Beam balance

today we adopt natural tactics[54]
strategies for greater importance
bigger better lit screen than anyone else
bright focused light to deter peering
put up a large print do not disturb sign
stuck firmly to the shut door I have you
balanced on the edge of movement and
the large digital clock on the wall reads
faster than any other clock how much
less time than you thought for speaking to me
glancing I see your hand raised to knock
you balance on the edge of your mind
I stand up interrupt you
do not catch your eye
my behaviour balances edges of
efficiency v human existence
until it's time (by my fast clock)
for me to go home
leaving a spare jacket on the back of the chair
while you work 5 real minutes longer

Punch Out the Air

In the quiet calm summer evening
pierrot in the park

when the dusk draws in the light and all the
carefully he picks something out from the

senses hold in breath the heightened
pavement edge he sings

smells on the air dry grass evening dew
to his MP3

the city is left for a weekend
forward then back then

in a country town luxury visit
dances towards the queue

and a call-in-sick Monday off go hear
fists punching the air

the town band in the park drowsy barely
hide from trouble

cooling sauntering air idling crossing
don't sit anywhere

sounds sights pleasure in this and that the band
round the curved patch

already playing strident breaching blast
city dust mocks planting

undercut by human murmurs clapping tune
hopping and singing in circles

after tune pleasure contented evening
tempt it temper a

send off one last Land of Hope and Glory
shaken heart machine

oh taking my breath away recall it
Tuesday 81° The Holloway Road

uprising punching out the air people stand
singing
crowd waits silent

a rolling crescendo of hearts tumult
unmelded sounds peel

of sound
away leaves hanging in heat from saplings

lights glow summer deepening dusk
rolling memory

unprepared for Sunday
drowns sounds emotions

evening songs
in the park blanket

for country hearts
of traffic roaring

switch to city and slows to gantry 50 40
heat punches the air

gyrations home to washes of city night
wave of hot tarmac

breathing air heat through
beep walk avoid shoulders go go the

buildings in and out up and down the streets
red lights run heat

buildings tower up cast shade hot pavement
squint in heat sun

skyscraper punctures air catches passing
shade wedge of cool

Strangers and Rising

humans shift interpret space proximity
with sounds that can only be heard under
second in hierarchy to supposed
silence within buildings - 'we are enslaved'
conditioned whisper in mournful humming
'release us, use us/ do not ever desert us/
fill us with movement/ we beckon you in/
do not pass our doors/ our integrity/
built by profiteers/ manipulated/
please see us we are/ growing older now/
we grow emptier/ floors and spaces change/
windows reset / designer lobby colours plans/
beyond gentle sighing/ make your day/
we insist/ demand/ determined claims/
morph our locations/ desires machines/
breathe give in and enter' -
and in the largest of atriums time
losing human sounds in the march
of daytime hours the night-time switches
open a door in silence to empty
lighting set upon by shadows
the building rejects and uneasy
this time cannot guarantee safety
no rights now the swaddling walls
express no audible wish just a swish
fire door pushed open falling shut
short sharp clack click the key turns echo
collect the forgotten papers nod
to the solitary night porter
saying nothing leave dare
dare not wait cannot wait to go out
and leave it breathing in its own pace

Shaking out the Syntagm[55]

Surely she has got used to death
now
quicksilver sunny deep shadow
after
eleven years and she twenty-six
then
her going marked year
by
year
I see her ghostly elegant stepping
down towards
the quartet playing Janacek
she salutes their nationalist welcome sits
amongst
them as they play they nod
across
their bows 'welcome - enjoy the music'
I
nearly
jump
out of
my seat groan
out loud
but choking keep my head
down
to cope of course
my heart threw arms
around
her crying at the same time
the embrace as close as lovers
movement harmony sympathy
when

I look up she has gone
leaving co-ordinates of more than one crossing
over

memory tingling peripheral senses
sententious Time
wearing great robes
wielding mallet seconds
pile driver minutes
seismic tremor hours
amniotic overbearing
losing people vista parabola
now

intimate working mechanisms
curves start stretching reference to the years
experience drifts any minute
now in

I do not notice the time is measured
out in

half-life unfocused eyes
blurring the plant and the filing cabinet
I think 'what you would have said?'
what if
what if that

if those arms truly embraced me
I would have known variable of recognition
that

too sharp moment
what I didn't and what you had
and what she lost and what you lost
then

my throat chokes
closes doors on malleable time
stop start stop start
up

Pellucid

amongst shadows footfalls
asking for directions fallacies
approaching shuns acid burns

first right then second left
turn your head twice first
crossing or diagonals x chemistry

crowds then empty streets
scattered people work and shards
this is no oil painting only rain

washes rushes through veins
hearing this inside out
I've half a mind to and

amongst shadows heartbeats
finding destinations half truths
distancing balancing perhaps

ETERNITY

City Dawn

Where dawn lights the glass
we know that heaven passes
                    through more than elucidating

Though south when sun is north east
         and the signs are least
                    well known through sleepiness
                                                  passing

After yawns gripped hands
         that quick glance at true sands
                    curtains alarms kettle rumbling

In traffic roseate cast
         adjusts eye fast past
                    and turn and sign sip adjusting

Through and through and through
         listening to proposals cue
                    replace the empty cup filling

Recursion

the metaphor of light?
reveal that all that glitters
people should be careful when buying
jewellery and given a course of
hard drives to repair the damage done
to this gyrus (or that)[56]

the metaphor of time
while away your time please
and we will take care of the hours
come crash with me or be my acrobat
angular damage or corner
one can be forgiven for thinking

the metaphor of place
the test material on the disc
read the readings to the 4th
childishly join the dots
process with functioning
fully functioning cycles

the metaphor of movement
you say you nicked your elbow by
completely missing the metaphorical angle?
head start and free fragments
incredulously watch her make
one swallow into her summer

her lists are endless (see web)
a straw a barricade a flood
of tears tumbling to earth
when I phone you say

I am having trouble finding you
I check my a-z for mountains
taken away my metaphors
and given me base real-time
that's tactile filed

"O you city ensued inhumanly"
I am growing ever more the same
the recursive link between us struggling
with two reluctant mutables
metaphors are cracked nuts
and here is the hammer which
crunches the hairlike scintilla
"eveningly" " and all the colours
have flown off" into
"an absence of blue leit-lines"[57]

Melody

collocation city breathlessness
theme sirens 3 am the spirit
leaven tokens bread is baked all night
packed into warehouse blinding flour dust
by heated ovens dough makers shout
through giant whirr whine high pitched
grinding
collocations split tin sandwich salt
on the edge of the city sounding
grace notes the rising hours they take from
thin tired ill paid desperate loaves
slices falling for sleep food and breath
collocations loaf pneuma spirit
city beats out coloratura
time and place collect patterns grace notes
close door run for the bus drop 5p
hear the acciaccatura jump
the mobile tune wheat from chaff threshing
by sound city skin and flesh wedged
swung lurching tight out of synch wheeling
coughs bravura city chest am
spittle never arrives breath not tune
voices underlay the background noise
traffic with variations rising
carrying city murmur – left hand
arpeggios – no grace notes - silence
rests dead time heartbeat beat measuring
the 19 bus take a deep breath in
city living metaphors etc
the bee the jar of honey (product
of more than one country) the salt mine
is the supermarket bag of salt

Washes of Light

Earth - I never touch it
pavements under my feet
with gold leaf or dusted over by feet of clay
the zone cracks fall into fragments
and positive combination
shadows fall on the concrete
cement rubble slabs besides
in two parts minus negative
interpolate north lights and poles
earth - I never touch it
my mum she has a window box
and waters plants from the market
ev-er-ry day
I tread on pavements every day
ev-er-y day
shadows lengthen before me then
harm emerges from fissures of narrow streets?
decaying or price-tagged thoroughfares
where time and drugs wreak shadows out
deadly combinations of earth
cadmium between our toes
lead mud in the rain
sour pockets of silt
I wouldn't touch it

Light - I never touch it
evening walking home sun warm on my face
briefly apricot house
the sun rests on my back
I open the door sun spins
caressing light falls
through time onto hall dust

and junk mail and bags left behind
then never getting in touch
travelling at this speed the pace threatens
time was halved for the duration
jacks or heads or dice parabola
combining the wasteland areas
intersections skills
signals now I understand
light I never touch it

Water – I never touch it –
Thames and Thames a few unseen springs
a few sewers outfalls a panegyric on barriers
until there are tears I haven't cried for years
it's a wonderful combination
science and human need
just don't increase the levels without
permission
and check with drain rods
I have visited rowed sailed worked driven
crossed watched walked over your bridges
and your grey flaccid wavelets
hold no fascination for me
who would care to eat salts of Maldon?
beyond the barrier wastes
was Tilbury pleased I was home?
unnoticed by tides in and out at
Fulham Hammersmith Barnes Chiswick Kew
looking down to Syon (near where I worked)
present marking the past with now
the way water cannot do
water I never touch it
and unreached beneath
foundations - I never touch them

Curvaceous and Enticing[58]

Continuum of process

Take a bite take a run look out! look out!
 a glance at the clock assures me of the
reason for all the panting it's relief
I just want to catch the 8.25
adjunct morning paper
adjunct avoid space occupying
adjunct no hope of a seat
adjunct mobile ringing said
'I want to change the process'
oblique silences confirm
our different agendas
point: buy shoes meet by surprise
point: hear about your night out
point: receive gas bill and gasp
we discuss the changes for hours
what shape is this dimension as
we combine the time it takes with
the room where we sit and eat drink
the number of words combining
scoring points embattled places
where is the person who can
rescue me from this humanly
without causing distress to

Uneven motivations

I have money in the bank
not a month goes by without
more money going in and
taken out I wish for more
money in so does the bank
so much so that this month they

charge me a lot more so they
can have much more that is mine
it's not a choice to stare so
long and hard magnifying
the sum column of figures
arabic numbers are so
curvaceous and enticing
the bank deeply responsive
to their allure sensual
sixes and sevens driving
forces behind the week's shop
I love irradiated fruit
figures attached delights
double choice half price buy three
dear slips of receipts the cost
is heartbreaking seen clearly
only with glasses and by
2-D card listen the bank
laughs electronic counting
machines adjust totals bring
carry forward patterns bags
chattering happy clicking
uneven motivations
pour in and out at the base
of the calm smooth tower soft
movements iced with deaf glass
staff present papers figures
are set to advantage why
ask for the resident poet
at the Bank Tower humbler
life incompatible with
over-riding cell systems
this complete expression of
you have and have it from me

Maintenance

just put a credit card in stop the wheel
then remove it when they read the meter
release the flow so I can afford food
I lift my bike through the first floor window
demolish the shed roof then 'these are weeds'
you said uprooting my free reclaimed plants
and the flow chart easy simple just watch
moving arrows flow in and out of doors
into large administrative buildings
and out again smaller this time I think
someone is pocketing the difference
there is no balance of input and loss
I turn my attention back to taller
more important buildings with energy
and lives matured in vitro and who
never respond what a maintenance diet

Weights

the young elegant black woman packed
with energy under a sleek firm skin
she is not for everyone determined
he tells her over and over to smile
can she avoid giving in shut him up
he thinks he has won made her obey him
now he has more weight but speaking over
the desire for power has cost insight
she has her future ahead of her
he has only his past behind him
she balances her weights assesses
she will wants goes for priority
African rhapsody polyglot
urban birthplace of plain English says
'it's only the French' I understand

she culturally knows the impact
the full weight of the demand repels
him over and over again oiled
perfumed skin of history now
darkened by desert sun now lit from
within hold out hold on hold up
she bears the weight of his demands weighs
heavily on her I look down when
your undelighted half muscle curve
set mouth shows clear measurements
she said I see death sits beside him
already his shadow weighs less than
a beam of light she sees it weighing
her words as I weigh his subverting
the conversation a discussion
of sexism we never win these tied
shadows of community are less
than the smallest avoirdupois though
with a slide moistened with saline
the cartographer may accrue time

Counterbalances

the survivor knocks at my door
I look beyond her to the houses opposite
then we talk for a long time agreeing
each day she sits on the bench by the grass
she has cut and dyed her hair
'I have over 20 cats now'
'you need to be vigilant'
'the rats have been dealt with'
'you seem well cared for
you're ok for money and food?'
she opens the book that she has under her arm
'this is the page'

showing me I read
'If the target image was preceded by a neutral
picture, the men were correct 90 per cent of the
time. But if it was preceded by a pornographic
image the subjects did no better than chance.
The "attentional rubbernecking", as the
researchers call it, lasted up to 800
milliseconds. The effect also occurs in women
and with violent images'[59]
'oh 800 milliseconds'
thinking what have I seen without realising it
is the survivor also subliminal
we have been talking for over 20 minutes
'have you got anything in the house
something you no longer need?'
I give her tins of cat food and money
the counterbalances must be attended to
you have also taken my time my self
you have taken the heat out of the hall
'something for nothing!'
laughing leaving
her shadow darkens across my feet
the memory does not stay
there is no weight to her argument
the visual weighs nothing
she will return
she does not

Soul Strobe

echoes of the dreadful night
intimately despair and darkness
and *loss* of inner light
search soul-less *eye*
the corners *longingly*
wishing for light without
harness the hope and light within
light source inexact
confusion of *light without* and
without light is common
much that is superficial
seen *combine* the two
with meeting *point*
easing a law of *perspective of light*
dividing lines between the two
harnessing reality or dislocations
stir thoughts and memories
construction of the viewpoint

You Are Here

watch *deepening* shadows
coloured by unease to *deepest* grey
the traffic *scarred* cornice
into the *inner* courtyard
young man sleeps *inert*
unnatural stillness *crumpled* limbs
stormy *dreams* a razor's edge
we look askance fleetingly *look*
hope layered such *base tags*
daylight creeps by with time
without warmth of sun or heart
coigned shadows the edge of hope
take a *quick* sip of time

eat the *crumbs* of light
lively moment *stumbling* block
or living *corner stone*
close *set* scoriations
builder's names *remember* me
close-up personal letters
and the *distant* targets
in the garden for the rescuers[60]
memories *leap* out of the air
white-faced after visiting your dying friend
white from the shadows *within*
bone tissue *resolving matter* into light
dark *within* our memories years
never seen by us from without
sometimes *overwhelming* light within
memory passing a shadow
across the iris of the *eye*
form informing
an inner *cloud* across the pupil sun
disjointed external *sudden* bangs
halts starts leaps *conjunctions*
immediate effect the tracks of love
stable effect *placed* in parts
we progress *from* A to B
from 9 *to* 10 am sub-totals
carried forwards brought forwards
is this what the burglar is after[61]
stealing away the *process* after
it was *stored* regulated
not backwards or forwards *just* today
or taken for *granted*
bringing the *parts* into the light
leaving them there

Triumphal

so what are my wages now?
earned life attributes do not
include grace promises with
half-life elision over
pitted surface scant nail grip
half-point this is killing me
fragments pictures fall torn
from my mind eternity
is more than the unfinished
negotiated matters
arising earning is this
from a human perspective
these conduction routes for fools
this random pattern yielding
blinding flash breaks time's contract
these are not destinations
this face these starting points of
illumination turning
away from eternity
lay my hands on anything
there is that vanishing point
again and the promise of
half-life after greater than
I have wanted to see you
so long half-life obscura
vision imagination
event reverse momentum
emotional tapestry
recognition renovate
grey into a shadow-burst
colour out of spun spectrum
at the right speed rock hard place

half-life hazy vantage point
multi-points statics copings
middle ground imbalance this
triumph of life processes

Embedding on[62]

the miserable multitude who had not
phantoms swept along by progress enslaved to
ageing fall and die weakest first unfinished
line 'Then, what is life? I cried -.'[63] encircling
show
in shade in sunlight repetition time voice
embedding particular person place how
hotfoot in pursuit life-thief spirit-breaker
memory-robber sight-snatcher ear-splitter
time space broken circle triumphs inhuman
without destination comprise whole city
forces beyond personal engagement not
divine condition *urbigena*[64] in this
sense breaking ranks keeping out of time this
line

Celebration

City year thread unwound
                    years with tares
thin pane between
voice and still
spirit and human
fruit and desert

and celebrate our sounds
                    shares and fears
voices flutter
take and give
inspire and utter
feather aspire

over my spirit bound
                              tensile bears
down-light years
way beyond
clear glass desert air
living and dust

residue grams and wounds
                              integers
skewed and veers
equals follows
dust lines and curves
patterns and drawn

The Desert in the City

'actions spatter deictics
here there and everywhere
fame has slipped up this time
"collective irrational exuberance"[65]
cough up and newly stain the
golden pavement red red red
as the blood stained pillow
on Kings Cross pavement
sputum of victims thrown down
here there and everywhere
daughters weep neither blood nor
tears on those it's as never
one hour later wash tears dust
alive dead without warning[66]

we hurry in dusty light
etiolated disperse
particles of sand between
blink there's dust in my eyes while
he sleeps in the corridor
stretched full length he slips slurs
folders fall like leaves shuffling
icons clicking chips ticking
while this machine is sleeping
voices footsteps startle means
nothing but his head is safe
cushioned laptop eyelids
close on SE1 taken
laid out to the Potters' Field[67]
foundations drawn from wind-blown
desert sands trace thin patterns[68]
veiling light on bitter glass'

Who Broke the Light?[69]

Glengall for fun
Salway on the run
picnics rubble
face up trouble
kicks in the teeth
hands on 'til death

did you set off at random and know
where you want to go or set off single
minded and get to better somewhere else?

4 bags each day
cruising up the
right to the heart
asking something
a complete split
of the paper
one is one side
the other side
of officials
'It's not easy
no chance he is
Glengall Glengall
careened by
particulates
just laid to park

taken away
saxon rat run[70]
children's faces
watch out for there's
between two sides
sheet after all[71]
the other is
Glengall's posse
banked up and
to read' can you -
'rather busy'[72]
The Isle of Dogs
westerlies and
never righted

Salway the better bet
clear the site and picnic
parole for the tea leaf
'he stole the pie miss' and
my heart in a straight line
from Stratford to St Paul's
leaving eleven sharp

notice round a child's neck
and collect on the way
pay for the breaks you done
you smashed his windscreen
more than eight miles all day
walking greeted warmly
by the 'old geezer in
a long black frock'[73] and crisps
chocolates and enough
to pay three times over
for the broken glass Look!
'Get them sparklers...they're real'[74]
all in a glass case " the
light has gone home by bus
the glass no longer counts
the shards cut or sparkle
or reveal or refract
come on! come in! The Dogs!
this way to the invisible
fun palace where glimpses of six
acres clothed in westwards sun
setting over the dull laid grass
of Sir John McDougall Gardens
that ravage the future seen through
darker glass behind where the walls
and moving stairs sway to the sounds
dreaming of past The Who and then
the smell of hot roasting chestnuts
where and when the people come by
not never the end of the tale

Caravanserai[75]

This evening in those lambent haven rooms
your words spoke to me of a hot desert wind
scoring rustling dry grasses remembering
the support of your luxuriant cushions
hot dusky cushions murmur echoes desire
swaying changing deciding silks slide me out
tasselled tentacles tip me in heated
paradisal fall degenerating to
sweat and dust all deadened by travelling
bright blue sky fretfully foretells bad weather
perspectives stretch out mind unendurably
blinded eyes search for fading and evening
unthinking unseeing shadowed shutters
blinking for comfort starving is more friendly
black dot in so much sanded grey streak and
stone
but the feelings of hot excitement unknot
pit and pitch of arriving messages here

shadows fall round the young man sitting
in the dust under the young plane tree
behind Euston with bedroll nervously
touching the pad over his eye
in dusk and sodium his unwashed
hands blood streaked the white bandage shows
glimpse of dried blood in a whiter light
ambulance man hovers by the rank
a policeman opens a notebook
holds a pen red perforates the dark
'Can you tell me your name?'
'Roy Gibbs'
'Thank you Roy, nice to meet you.

Got anywhere to go Roy?'
Cubits and amulets measure real
time silence before his clear reply
'There's my sister 'Gina'
The bus is due any minute now
edges govern sight and sound
'Do you have a phone Roy?'
'That's what they took'
'Shall I phone 'Gina for you Roy?'
Roy nervous touches his painful eye
'Have you got 'Gina's number Roy?'

'Hello is that 'Gina? Do you have a brother
'Gina?
'Listen to me 'Gina can you pick him up'
'Camden yes'
'Can you get on a bus Roy?'
Roy is too far away to measure
'OK, Roy! Roy!
'Gina will come for you.
You won't move will you Roy? Just stay here
she will be here in half an hour'

Radios call they are on the move
the ambulance man gets in his cab
the policeman goes to his motorbike
listens to voices instructions waits
stares towards the dusty road junction
the bus is coming
and the now lit windows are too few
to catch the mottled sitting figure
in shaded dust beneath the plane tree
Roy and 'Gina disappear away
no light nothing personal pulling

past the 5 star hotel the doorman
stands in the window facing the street
talking by mobile to the woman
right outside in a waiting taxi
derelict hospital
the brand new hospital
this is my last portal
into the centre now

Afterword

'Shades of Light' is an exploration of a city poetic. The poem is divided into six sections, the title of each is adapted from Petrarch's 'Trionfi' or 'Triumphs' begun around 1334. The idea of the 'Triumphs' has been re-interpreted both poetically and artistically over a long period of time; including by Sir Thomas More, Holbein and Mary Sidney, Countess of Pembroke who retranslated Petrarch's 'Triumph of Death' as an exploration of personal grief for the loss of her brother Sir Philip Sidney who died of wounds in the Low Countries in 1586. Shelley was much inspired by the Triumphs and wrote his own addition 'The Triumph of Life' in 1822. This was the poem he was working on when he died, leaving it unfinished. Geoffrey Hill, more recently, has written The Triumph of Love.

The sections of 'Shades of Light' are: Love, Discipline, Death, Fame, Time and Eternity. The structure of the poem is, more explicitly, The Triumph of Love over the Poet; The Triumph of Discipline over Love and so on. In a contemporary exploration of a city poetic, Petrarch's 'Triumphs' have the additional relevance of a humanist viewpoint. Writing poetry about crowded urban spaces, of necessity, requires focus on a poetic interpretation of people's lives if a city poetic is not to be overwhelmed by topography, architecture, statistics, history, politics or sociology. And how does the human survive the inanimate (though rapidly changing) structure of the city? This poem attempts to explore the humanist viewpoint without being anthropocentric. The section 'Fame' has been written with Adobe Indesign software.

This poem explores the construction of a poetic city space. This includes the process whereby the artist or poet makes strange something which is familiar (ostranenie) so that it is really seen once again. Projection is a crucial aspect of ostranenie and also has a bearing on how 'projected' is understood within a poetic framework. The term 'projection' is linked to Roman Jakobson's theory of 'Poetic Function'. 'Projection' has several properties but within the theory of Formalist function it suggests a sense of movement which this poem explores as a structure for a city poetic. If the artist is able to project a visual image that is not literal, then the poet can project words in the same way. Meaning can arise from a collocation of metonymic phrases – the meaning arises from phrase added to phrase – parts of meaning added to parts of meaning. This can interpret city poetic space. Deictics also give a strong sense of time, place and space; and perhaps this is the heart of a city poetic. The city with all its energy and activity – lines crossing, junctions – real and influential - is combined with the people, the energy and the travelling through.

ENDNOTES

[1] Graham-Rowe, D. (2006) Gamers Turn Cities into Playgrounds: Ditch the Sofa and hit the Streets in a Gaming Revolution where you can chase Pac-Man or play Tom for real New Scientist Vol.186, No.2503, pp26/7

[2] Classical Greek meaning: thread.

'Two or more players, who may never have met, speed through a city leaving a virtual trail behind them that is plotted on their mobile phone screens. There is one rule: you can't cross your own trail or that of the other player, so the basic tactic is to try and encompass or corral your opponent, forcing him or her to cross a trail and lose the game' (Graham-Rowe op.cit.).

[3] Logic Gates or logic circuits: 'The basic switching circuits of gates used in digital computers and other digital electronic devices. The three basic logic circuits are the AND, OR, and NOT circuits (A Dictionary of Science, Eds. John Daintith and Elizabeth Martin, 2005 Oxford, OUP).

[4] Eidometropolis – for an exploration and definition of this term see: James Chandler and Kevin Gilmartin in Romantic Metropolis 2005 Cambridge, Cambridge University Press. The term describes how a city is perceived, deriving from the Greek eidos meaning idea – how the city is culturally explored as an idea – the city as ideated.

[5] Mrs Gilpin is John Gilpin's wife – she features in the poem by William Cowper (1731-1800) 'The Diverting History of John Gilpin; Showing How He Went Farther Than He Intended, And Came Safe Home Again'.

[6] This is a direct quotation from Brecht's Journals.

[7] This is a reference to Plath, S Ariel 1964 London, Faber 'Morning Song' p11

[8] *Lord Morley's Tryumphes of Fraunces Petrarke* (1971) (Ed.) D.D. Carnicelli, Trans. Lord Morley, Cambridge MA, Harvard University Press; from the section 'The Tryumph of Love' p101

[9] Ibid. p 102

[10] Petrarch trans. by E.H.Wilkin, op.cit. p26

[11] This poem arises from T.S.Eliot's 'The Waste Land': 'III: The Fire Sermon' with the lines on the typist:

'The typist home at teatime, clears her breakfast, lights

Her stove, and lays out food in tins' et seq.
Collected Poems 1909-1962 (1974) London, Faber.
The grey page headings in this section are taken from: 'Red Tape'(RT). This is the journal of Women civil servant secretarial staff; and AWK (The Association of Women Clerks). The quotations have been chosen as the dates of these journals, housed in the TUC Library at The London Metropolitan University, coincide with the dates that T.S.Eliot originally wrote The Waste Land (1922).

[12] from the classical Greek: 'tupto' – 'τυπτω' to strike

[13] An inspiration for this was from Andrew Crozier's poem 'Survival Kit' in All Where Each Is (1985) London, Fiona Allardyce

[14] unattributed quote from Zsa Zsa Gabor, taken from a women's weekly magazine around 1980.

[15] The specific months and some of the details of these events relate to the suppression of Syon Abbey, Bridgettine Monastery, during the reformation: the dispersal; November 1556, re-establishment under Queen Mary; May 1559, final dissolution and exile of the religious sisters to Europe.

[16] These lines are taken from: COCKBURN, J.S. et al (Eds.) (1969) [online] Religious Houses: House of Bridgettines in A History of the County of Middlesex: Vol. I: Physique, Archaeology, Domesday pp182-191 Available at: http://www.british-history.ac.uk/report.aspx?compid=22119 [Accessed 12 October 2010]

[17] EASTMAN, J et al. Trauma: London Medics (2005) BBC1 television, broadcast 20.00-20.30; 28 July 2005

[18] ARISTOTLE Poetics p53 (1999) Cambridge MA, Harvard University Press

[19] This is a quotation from Brecht's poem: 'To Those Born Later' in Poems, 1913-1956, Eds. John Willett and Ralph Manheim (1979) London, Methuen, p318

[20] In classical Greece the rhapsode's profession was distinguished and well paid. It consisted of reciting poetry from memory in public, emphasising the effects on the audience.

[21] This poem derives from Peirce's system as detailed by Floyd Merrell in Signs for Everybody: Chaos, Quandaries, and Communication (2000). Each line attempts to fulfil a box on the

diagrammatic representation of Peirce's system of signs, see Chapter Three:'How Signs Proliferate'. Each stanza of the poem is described by one of Peirce's categories as per the above designation. Peirce describes 9 signs (three rows of three) which can be combined:
Qualsign, Icon, Term/Word (111/211/311)
Sinsign, Index, Proposition/Sentence (211/221/222)
Legisign, Symbol, Argument/Text/Narrative (311/321/322)
Additional categorisations are: 331/332/333 (pp37-54).
These categories are combined with qualities of firstness, secondness and thirdness. This theory is demonstrated by using 3 numbers to define the nature of the communication. Accordingly, the example of the first stanza of the poem given below, demonstrates this construction:

some kind of	111
and there	211
from within and without	221
I walk in shaded triangles	222
and into light	311
(I think this is a God given place)	333
and palaver and paloma	321
and imprint	322
turning	211
just to see the shadows	331
of arches shifting	322
I walk past pillars	332

In the poem the '333' lies within the text as a whole, the whole poem but also within the poem itself. For example see line 6 in each stanza which jumps out of sequence to 333. This is why it is in brackets, it has arrived before its logical time.

[22] Mr Eliot can you calculate our annual leave? [see RT (1923) Vol.XII, No. 138, p198], the full quote is:
'For instance, if one-eighth of the staff are allowed away at once, and leave is divided into eight periods of three weeks each from April 23rd to October 15th, then where there is, say, a total staff of 1,600, 200 of the staff would be away at the same time. The first year this scheme is put into force the senior women choose

the period they want, but the next year they automatically have to take their leave three periods on. Thus it works out that all the staff in due course get a decent leave period.'

[23] These two words are taken from Dame Edith Sitwell's poem 'Street Song' Collected Poems (1957) London, Macmillan & Co. pp277/8. 'Starless Night' reflects some of the mood and rhythms of this poem.

[24] This is the London Bombings of 7th July 2005. There were 52 deaths and over 700 injured. 7 deaths were at Aldgate tube station, 6 deaths at Edgware Road tube station, 26 deaths at Russell Square tube station and 13 deaths on the double decker bus that was bombed in Tavistock Square, near Kings Cross. Source – BBC News: http://www.bbc.co.uk/news/uk-11511461 accessed: 11.30am, 19.11.10

[25] 'A Mirror Neuron is one that is active when the individual whose brain it is in is engaged in some action or experiencing some sensation or emotion, and also when that particular action, sensation or emotion is being observed in someone else's'. 'Neurology: Empathy with others seems to be due to a type of brain cell called a mirror *'neuron'* (2005) (No Author) Economist Vol.375, No. 8426, pp81/82

[26] This quote and the subsequent one are from 'The Triumph of Death translated out of Italian by the Countesse of Pembroke. The first chapter' (in The Collected Works of Mary Sidney Herbert, Countesse of Pembroke (1998) Eds. Margaret P. Hannay et al. Oxford, Clarendon Press pp276 and 274 respectively.

[27] This is a different look at some ideas explored by Dame Edith Sitwell in her poem 'Street Acrobat' ibid. pp358-360. Dame Edith Sitwell visited Skid Row when she gave a lecture tour in America: 'There were but few beings who once had been women, and these would have seemed sexless as the dead, had not, once in a while, a child been seen pressed down among the fluttering banners of its misery...Blown along the street, they had a special mode of locomotion. In a series of articles on Skid Row, "The Legion of the Damned", that appeared in The Mirror of Los Angeles, Mr Lou Larkin wrote: "They don't walk. They keep falling forward. It is a slow muscleless movement dependent almost entirely on the law of gravity...the torso is

allowed to fall forward, the right knee joint locks, supporting the body, which then rocks slightly to the right. This movement lifts the left leg from the ground. Free, it swings forward another twenty inches and so on. Veteran bums will tell you that this mode of locomotion requires less energy than standing in one place"' Edith Sitwell (1965) Taken Care Of: An Autobiography London, Hutchinson.

[28] This is a reference to the interview with the nurse on duty at the Accident and Emergency of St Thomas's Hospital, London the day of the 7.7. bombings. EASTMAN, J et al (Producers) (2005) Trauma – London Medics BBC1 television, broadcast, 28th July 2005

[29]'Michael Shermer (2006) The Political Brain Scientific American Vol.295, No. 1, p36 suggests that MRI scans show that the political brain minimises rationality and reasoning in favour of emotions which reinforce confirmation bias 'whereby we seek and find confirmatory evidence in support of already existing beliefs and ignore or reinterpret disconfirmatory evidence'

[30] Taken from a proverb 'drive gently over the stones' meaning to take care or be overconfident. It is one of the few proverbs that have a basis in city images. See Oxford Dictionary of Proverbs Oxford, OUP 2004

[31] This is the title of a poem by Brecht from Bertolt Brecht Poems Part One 1913-1928 (1976) (translated by John Willett and Ralph Manheim) London, Eyre Methuen, III The Impact of Cities 1925-1928, p159.

[32] The story behind this is the Department for Transport has released figures showing a 19% increase in death or serious injury to cyclists from April to June of this year. This is compared to the same period in 2008. Add to that a rise of 7% to minor injuries. see website: www.londoncyclist.co.uk [Accessed: 7.3.2011]

[33] This line and the subsequent 5 lines are paraphrased from Brecht on Theatre: 1933-1947 (translated by John Willett) London, Methuen, 1964 p124 from the section entitled 'The Street Scene: A Basic Model for an Epic Theatre' Brecht is exploring how the actor interprets an actual scene: 'Another essential element in the street scene is that the demonstrator

should derive his characters entirely from their actions. He imitates their actions and so allows conclusions to be drawn about them.'

[34] Quotation from Brecht on Theatre: 1933-1947 (translated by John Willett) London, Methuen, 1964 p122

[35] Op.cit. p122

[36] Bertolt Brecht Poems Part One 1913-1928 (1976) (Translated by John Willett and Ralph Manheim) London, Eyre Methuen p131 and p 141. These are words from the titles of two sections of poems: 'Ten Poems from a Reader for Those who Live in Cities' and 'Poems Belonging to a Reader for Those who Live in Cities'

[37] Much of the content of these last lines of the poem are an interpretation of Brecht's 'Alienation Effect' with an attempt to interpret poetically, the gap between the poet (who is now dead) and the reader.

[38] This poem attempts to demonstrate an experiment with the idea of a negative synechdoche/metonym which suggests that the parts do not represent the whole.

[39] The arrows are used: → to denote memory moving forward through the recalled action and ← to denote the emotional dragging into the past through the flashback recall.

[40] Allen Fisher places a comma at the beginning of a line to indicate a breath in - see *Gravity* (2004) Cambridge, Salt Publishing. Examples are: pp20, 21, 22 (in 'Ballin' the Jack') and p36('Atkins Stomp'). In this poem the dots indicate an exhalation.

[41] Kineme is to kinesics as phoneme is to linguistics – the smallest unit of non-speech language – for example body movement.

[42] 'once an iPod is plugged into a computer, slurp.exe takes just 65 seconds to rifle through its hard drive, home in on all Excel, pdf and Word files, and copy them to the iPod hard drive…' Cast-off Spacesuit to go into orbit (2005) New Scientist Vol.186, No. 2505, p29.

[43] See Aristotle's The Art of Rhetoric (1991) London, Penguin, pp245-261 (p245).

[44] This is from the final sentence of Aristotle's Rhetoric: 'An asyndetic [co-ordinated clauses or phrases without explicit

conjunctions or connectives – see Wales, Dictionary of Stylistics p33)] ending is appropriate for the speech, so that it should be a peroration, not an oration: "I have spoken, you have heard, you have the facts, judge" [quoted from Lysias Against Eratosthenes, last words].

[45] The layout of this poem derives from Jakobson's diagrammatic representation of a prose poem by Paul Klee Jakobson has interpreted Klee's writing as a diagram representing two mountains and a valley. The first mountain is: 'bright mountain'/'negation of negation; the valley is: 'dusky valley'/'affirmation of negation' and the second mountain is: 'clear mountain'/'affirmation of affirmation' (see Jakobson, 1987 Language in Literature pp497-503).

[46] This is adapted from: An Essay on the Art of Ingeniously Tormenting originally written in the early 18th century by Jane Collier (2006) Oxford, OUP.

[47] See 'Supraconscious Turgenev in Jakobson (1987) Language in Literature Cambridge, MA, Harvard University Press,pp262-266)

[48] See Jakobson (1987) Language in Literature Cambridge, MA, Harvard University Press, p63

[49] Narrative controls mood and point of view through the use of direct speech, does this occur in poetry too? In Allen Fisher's Bel Air (see Gravity,pp 44-52) he uses verbs suddenly one after the other and then does not use them at all. Narrative can also be altered through the use of verbs, adverbs (especially deictics of time and place) and other parts of speech bringing the writer and reader closer together – or further apart.

[50] See The Painter in Allen Fisher's 'Bel Air' (Gravity (2004) Cambridge, Salt Publishing).

[51] This is a quote from Jakobson's chapter on Turgenev ibid. p262-66.

[52] This is a derivation of Jakobson on Turgenev ibid. p262-66.

[53]Allen Fisher in 'Bel Air', instead of using word pictures, has introduced the Painter who does not shape the poem but is described by him.

[54] MOTLUK, A (2006) Motluk 'Got a Minute? New Scientist Vol.190, No.2557, pp46-49:

'Tips for surfing the wave of interruptions:

• Get a bigger monitor. A Microsoft study found it helped people work up to 44 per cent faster — one of the biggest boosts to productivity yet.
• Put up a clear "do not disturb" sign, or an obvious signal that you are busy. Insist that your colleagues respect it.
• Rearrange your office furniture so your desk faces away from the flow of people, so no one can catch your eye.
• Always stand up to talk to someone who is interrupting you, so they know what they're doing.
• Put a big clock in plain view of visitors and check it while you are talking.
• Be prepared: if an interruption is likely to take longer than 2 minutes, add it to your to-do list and go back to what you were already doing.
• Keep a notebook open and write down what you are doing as soon as you are interrupted.
• Cutting 2 centimetres off the front legs of a chair makes it just uncomfortable enough to keep visits short'.

[55] In this poem the deictics of place and time – and perhaps even of space = time + place - are selected out to the right-hand margin. This highlights how the deictics construct an axis of their own. The text tends to be read on the left-hand side only and the meaning is shifted to enhance the sense of dislocation between life and the imagined.
[56] See Alexandrov 'Literature, Literariness, and the Brain (2007). He reviews work done on the left and right hemispheres of the brain: 'it is possible to hypothesize that creating or reading a sonnet requires the full abilities of both hemispheres, while reading or writing something mundane, like a set of directions, requires the left hemisphere but only limited aspects of the right' (Comparative Literature online version of article, p7). See also: New Scientist 'What Metaphor? 16.4.2005 Vol. 186, No. 2495 p18. This article suggests that if the brain is damaged in the area called the 'left angular gyrus' the person cannot understand proverbs. Someone who cannot understand proverbs cannot understand metaphor.

[57] The quotations are from Aljagrov (pseudonym for Roman Jakobson) 'How Many Fragments Have Scattered' (1992 My Futurist Years compiled and edited by Bengt Jangfeldt and Stephen Rudy (translator) New York, Marsilio Publishers p253

[58] Within a city poetic there is a poetic attempt to measure force, impact, cause, effect, stasis, movement and of course energy. The following five sections explore some of these forces. This city poem attempts to explore human existence within a space that is both given and powerful and is imposed on the humans within it. This is an unequal relationship which arises because changes occur without apparent direct cause and effect. The only collective impetus might arise from vested outside interests (profit, for example) not the expressed collective human wish. Somehow, in the symbiotic relationship between the vested interests and the population there is a continuum of process which is unevenly motivated and maintained and can be expressed in terms of weights and counterbalances. This indicates, that for a city poetic there is an inevitable leaning towards a scientific model (but see St Augustine: 'each individual in this community is driven by his passions to pursue his private purposes. Unfortunately, the objects of these purposes are such that no one person (let alone, the world community) can ever be wholly satisfied….The result is that the city of man remains in a chronic condition of civil war . Hence, there is always the oppression of those who fail by those who succeed. The vanquished succumb to the victorious, preferring sheer survival and any kind of peaceful settlement to their own continued hegemony – even to liberty itself' (City of God (1958) Book XVIII, Chapter 2, New York, Image Books p 392). There is also a debt to Allen Fisher here. His poems Place and Gravity explore place, space, time. He refers to an earlier version of Gravity as gravity as a consequence of shape (see Preface to Brixton Fractals 1985 in Gravity (2004) p xii).

[59] These lines are quotations are from an article in New Scientist 'Keep Your Eyes on the Road' 20 August 2005 Vol. 187, No. 2513 p6.

[60] This is a reference to Postman's Park and The Memorial to Heroic Self Sacrifice situated at Little Britain, City of London just behind St Paul's Cathedral. It was established in the late

19th century to commemorate the heroic deaths of those people of London who lost their own lives whilst saving the lives of others. There is a 'Wall of Heroes' with tiles to commemorate the person and the heroic act they performed.

[61] There are a number of poems in Gravity by Allen Fisher (2004) which mention 'the burglar'. Examples include 'Bel Air' pp 44- 52 and many of the poems in the sequence 'Buzzards and Bees' both in Gravity pp124-146.

[62] Shelley's 'The Triumph of Life' is unfinished.

[63] Quoted from the last line of Shelley's 'The Triumph of Life' in *Shelley's Poetical Wo*rks (1932) London, OUP pp503-516.

[64] see David Jones The Anathémata Section III 'Angle-Land' p112 footnote: Quoting Gilbert Sheldon: 'The Latin name Urbigena, city-born, is disguised as Urien [as in the Welsh Romance of Taliesin]'. There is not an easily spoken word which describes city-dweller in the modern english language.

[65] Adair Turner, Chairman of the FSA; speech given to the FSA 14.7.10 at 'The Future of Finance Conference' in London.

[66] From The Night Litany: see Poor Clare Monastery, Arkley. This community used to be based at Notting Hill where they had, and still have, a vocation to pray for city dwellers. The Litany is said during the night.

[67] The Potters Field is the burial ground for strangers. Listed in Hastings (HASTINGS, J, (1924) Dictionary of the Bible Edinburgh, T&T Clark) under 'Akeldama': 'The name of the 'potter's field' [see Acts, Ch. I v.19], purchased for the burial of strangers with the blood-money returned by Judas [see NT St Matthew, Ch 27, v.3] There is a Potters Field in London SE1 in Lambeth.

[68] 'Possible sources [of dust] included volcanic ash from an eruption on 26 February 2000 in Iceland, or dust from large sandstorms over the Sahara. A combination of atmospheric transport modelling using the Lagrangian dispersion model NAME, an analyses of satellite imagery and observational data from Mace Head has shown that the most likely origin of the episode was long range transport of dust from the Sahara region of North Africa' (RYALL, D B et al. (2002) The origin of high particulate concentrations over the United Kingdom, March 2000 Atmospheric Environment Vol. 36, pp1363-1378).

[69] This poem is based on the incident that Joan Littlewood records in her autobiography. (LITTLEWOOD, J (2003) *Joan's* Book: The Autobiography of Joan Littlewood London, Methuen) The children she worked with marched to St Pauls' in order to collect money from the public to pay for a broken windscreen. The reference to the 'fun palace' arises from Sir Cedric Price's design for a large public building that was entirely moveable inside so that it could perform many functions. It was never built. Joan Littlewood identified an unused 6 acre site on the Isle of Dogs for it.

[70] Angel Lane is the old Saxon route which the Anglo-Saxons used to avoid the Romans who controlled London as an invading force.

[71] This is a reference to Saussure's example of how the signifié and the signifiant cannot be separated as they are like two sides of a sheet of paper. (Course in General Linguistics(1966) p113: 'Language can be compared with a sheet of paper: thought is the front and the sound the back; one cannot cut the front without cutting the back at the same time; likewise in language, one can neither divide sound from thought nor thought from sound;' Unfortunately politicians seem to get round this problem. Joan Littlewood met with immediate opposition to her plans for a fun palace, the mayors and councillors of different boroughs teamed up to ensure that the plan completely failed.

[72] These are the quoted words of Cedric Price see 'Joa*n's B*ook' p702

[73] Op. cit. p759

[74] Op. cit. p760

[75] Caravanserai is originally a Persian word meaning caravan and palace or inn, usually with a large courtyard. It describes accommodation for traders brought merchandise to cities. The word 'paradise' is also a Persian word from pairi (meaning 'around') and daeza (meaning 'wall').